The
Guinea Pig

An Owner's Guide To

A HAPPY HEALTHY PET

Howell Book House

Hungry Minds, Inc.
New York, NY • Cleveland, OH • Indianapolis, IN

Howell Book House
Hungry Minds, Inc.
909 Third Avenue
New York, NY 10022
www.hungryminds.com

For general information on Hungry Minds books in the U.S., please call our
Consumer Customer Service department at 800-762-2974. In Canada, please
call (800) 667-1115. For reseller information, including discounts and premium
sales, please call our Reseller Customer Service department at 800-434-3422.

Library of Congress Cataloging-in-Publication Data available upon request.

ISBN: 0-87605-527-7

Manufactured in the United States of America

12 11 10 9 8
Second Edition

Series Director: Kira Sexton
Book Design: Michele Laseau
Cover Design: Michael Freeland
Photography Editor: Richard Fox
Illustration: Bryan Towse
Photography:
  Front cover photo by Jean Miele / Stock Market
  Back cover photo by Ron Kimball Studio
  ARBA: 33, 34, 35, 36, 37
  Joan Balzarini: 10, 65, 84, 91, 93, 104, 111
  Mary Bloom: 100
  Cheryl Primeau: 48, 114
  David Schilling: 31, 54, 73, 76, 95, 101, 115
  Renee Stockdale: 2–3, 5, 6, 8, 9, 12, 13, 14, 15, 19, 24, 25, 30, 38–39, 40,
    41, 42, 43, 44, 46, 51, 56, 57, 58, 59, 60, 62, 68, 69, 72, 74, 79, 80, 83, 85,
    86, 90, 92, 96, 102, 103, 105, 107, 109, 110, 113, 118
  Bruce Webb: 21, 28, 98–99
Page creation by: Hungry Minds Indianapolis Production Department

Contents

About

part one

Guinea Pigs

External Features of the Guinea Pig

Ear

Eye

Nose

Foot

Rump

chapter 1

The **History**
of the
Guinea Pig

The sweet, simple little animal we know as the guinea pig—or cavy, as he is also known—has a rich and exotic past.

The guinea pig's history begins with the earliest rodent fossils from the Paleocene era, around 57 million years ago. Different rodent families evolved from these very early mammals until, 20 million years ago, during the mid-Miocene era, the Caviidae family of rodents appeared in South America. From these ancient species, the modern guinea pig evolved.

The Natural Guinea Pig

The scientific name for the domestic guinea pig is *Caviidae porcellus*. The guinea pig belongs to the cavia genus, of which there are

5

four other members, all wild cavies still living in South America. These wild relatives are found in the grasslands and scrub of South America, as well as in desert climates and the high altitudes of the Andes Mountains.

The guinea pig is a rodent and is related to such diverse creatures as the mouse, beaver, porcupine and capybara. Like most rodents, the guinea pig is an herbivore, or plant eater. His front teeth, or incisors, grow continuously as do the incisors of all rodents, and must be worn down through gnawing.

The domesticated guinea pig has a rich and exotic history.

Most guinea pigs—domestic and wild—share the same physical form. They have a round, cobby body and a large head that makes up about one-third of the animal's length. The eyes and ears are big. The hind feet have three clawed toes, while the front feet have four toes with claws. The guinea pig has no tail.

Both wild and domestic guinea pigs are known for their ability to reproduce quickly. Females are capable of bearing young at one month old. Gestation takes nearly two to three months in guinea pigs, depending on the species. Litters usually consist of three or four pups.

The wild cavy cousins of the domestic guinea pig live in social groups called herds, in which they use a series of squeals, squeaks and squawks to communicate with one another. To keep peace within the herd, cavies establish an order of dominance. A male cavy becomes the dominant animal in the group and is the only one allowed to mate with the females.

Because wild cavies have few physical defenses against predators, they use their social groupings for protection. Members of a wild herd create trails between their burrows so they can easily run for cover when danger approaches. They also warn each other of lurking predators with vocalizations and body language that other cavies can understand.

The Guinea Pig in South America

Thousands of years ago, the native peoples of South America ate wild cavies. The Incas eventually domesticated the animal around 5000 B.C. They used cavies for food and in religious ceremonies. The Spaniards who arrived in Peru in the sixteenth century were the first Europeans to lay eyes on this species of animal.

> **GUINEA PIG VOCABULARY**
>
> **cavy:** guinea pig
>
> **boar:** male guinea pig
>
> **sow:** female guinea pig
>
> **herbivorous:** plant-eating

After the Spanish conquest of the Inca empire, Dutch merchants brought cavies back to Europe. They became popular as pets among aristocrats in Europe during the 1600s, in large part because Queen Elizabeth I of England kept one as a pet.

Over the next 300 years, Europeans began deliberately breeding guinea pigs for different traits. In the nineteenth century, British immigrants brought some of these specially bred guinea pigs to America, and the cavy fancy in the United States was set to flourish.

Guinea Pigs in the United States

In the United States, the specialized breeding of guinea pigs for exhibition began in the early 1900s. In

1910, a group called the National Pet Stock Association was formed to govern the breeding of small mammals such as rabbits, guinea pigs and hamsters. In 1923, the organization changed its name to the American Rabbit and Cavy Breeders Association, and it dealt only with rabbits and guinea pigs.

Cavy breeders opted to leave the American Rabbit and Cavy Breeders Association in 1952 and formed their own organization called the American Cavy Breeders Association (ACBA). The American Rabbit and Cavy Breeders Association became the American Rabbit Breeders Association (ARBA) and began dealing only with rabbits.

The breeding of guinea pigs has been associated with rabbit breeding from the very beginning.

Eventually, the American Cavy Breeders Association reunited with the American Rabbit Breeders Association, and now the ACBA functions as a division of the ARBA. To this day, the ARBA is still the governing body for the guinea pig fancy in this country.

The Guinea Pig Today

The guinea pig is a popular pet in the United States because of his affectionate nature and easy care. Guinea pig fanciers breed their animals to exhibit in events around the country. The guinea pig has also thrived as a companion, and millions of children—and adults—have developed relationships with this sweet little creature.

In North America and Europe, the guinea pig's main function is as a pet, show and research animal. However, in other parts of the world, the guinea pig serves different purposes.

In South America, where the guinea pig originated, the animal is still used for food and in religious ceremonies. Known as the "cuy" in South American culture, people of all social classes eat the guinea pig because of the high protein content of his meat. Guinea pig meat is also eaten in some urban areas in North America where Hispanic populations are high.

The guinea pig is related to other rodents, including hamsters.

In small Indian villages in the Andes Mountains, guinea pigs are raised in the home, usually in the kitchen. Here the inhabitants of the home live in close quarters with the animals. Raising guinea pigs in the home is not limited to small villages. In large cities such as Lima, Peru and La Paz, Bolivia, guinea pigs are also raised at home. However, commercial breeding of guinea pigs for food is becoming more common.

The guinea pig is an important factor in the economies of several South American countries. Even his manure, a byproduct of the commercial guinea pig meat trade, is used as a fertilizer.

9

In Western society, the guinea pig also serves another function: that of laboratory animal. In the English language, the term guinea pig is associated with experimentation because the animals are popular subjects in scientific research. Specially bred guinea pigs are sold to laboratories, where they are used to study human disease. Approximately 500,000 guinea pigs a year are used in scientific research.

Guinea Pig Lore
WHAT'S IN A NAME?

There are different theories about how the cavy came to be called the guinea pig. Some historians speculate that since cavy meat tastes somewhat like pork, people

began to refer to the animal as a pig. The term "guinea" may be a mispronunciation of Guyana, a South American country where the animals were acquired by European traders.

Another theory asserts that these small animals were sold by Dutch merchants for one guinea, an old coin once used in Europe. Because people thought the little animals resembled pigs, the term "guinea pig" evolved.

A LINK TO THE SPIRITS

In South America, the guinea pig is believed to have great powers of

In America today, the guinea pig is a popular companion to adults and children alike.

healing. In Indian culture, the guinea pig is used to diagnose and remove sickness from the bodies of ailing patients. It is also thought that the guinea pig has the power to appease the supernatural and thus remove illness from the body.

One tradition calls for the animal to be set free in the Ecuadorian Andes. A garment from the sick person is draped over the guinea pig, and pieces of ribbon and yarn are attached to the cloth. It is believed that the guinea pig will remove the illness from the person through the clothing and then take the disease to a place where it can do no harm. In order for the guinea pig to do this, the family of the ill person must take the guinea pig to a sacred place in the Andes called Quinchi Urco, where he is set free to live among the wild cavies that still roam there.

The guinea pig is also used in a number of other rituals in South America. It is believed that the guinea pig can help people pass from one stage of life to another. The animal also plays a large part in the celebration of Patron Saints Day.

Today in the United States, the guinea pig has an equally important function: beloved pet and companion.

chapter 2

Guinea Pigs
as **Pets**

The Right Pet for You?

Compared to a dog, a guinea pig is a fairly easy pet to own. Guinea pigs don't need to go on long walks every day or be taken to obedience school. The owner of a guinea pig can leave his or her pet alone for several hours a day and not have to worry about the animal needing bathroom breaks.

On the other hand, guinea pigs are not maintenance-free pets. They are social creatures who need a lot of love and attention, along with quality care.

To determine whether or not a guinea pig would be a good pet for you, think about your lifestyle. Will your job, school or other commitments allow you to set aside time every day to spend with your guinea pig? Guinea pigs need daily interaction in order to meet their emotional needs. If you must leave a guinea pig alone for many hours each day, you should probably have two guinea pigs so they can keep each other company. Are you willing to make the commitment to spend several hours a day with your guinea pig, or to take on the responsibility of owning two of them?

Guinea pigs are social creatures who need attention and quality care from their owners.

Guinea pigs also need daily exercise. Your guinea pig will be confined to a cage or hutch most of the time. Will you be able to let her out each day for supervised activity?

You'll need to scrub your guinea pig's cage every week or so, and clean out the soiled areas every day. You'll also have to feed your pet and make sure she has fresh, clean water. Can you work these tasks into your schedule?

Think about where you live. Do you have room to house a guinea pig, either outside or inside your home? Keep in mind that a guinea pig needs an ample-sized cage that will keep her safe from other pets and predators, and plenty of room to romp during supervised play times.

If you have children, are they old enough to learn how to handle the guinea pig properly and treat her with respect? Very young children cannot be expected to understand that a guinea pig needs to be held a certain way, and that a guinea pig should not be picked up without adult supervision.

If your children are older, will you still take responsibility for the pet, despite their promises to do so? Even though they have the best of intentions, most children do not have the attention span required for the care of a guinea pig, who may live as long as seven years.

If you decide to give your child the temporary responsibility of caring for the guinea pig, you should always be there to monitor the pet's well-being. No child should be given unsupervised responsibility for an animal. Children cannot be expected to recognize signs of illness in a guinea pig, or to be able to judge the guinea pig's well-being. An adult should always be the pet's primary caregiver. Any other arrangement could result in harm to the pet, either through neglect or inexperience on the part of the child. And when the child eventually loses interest, it will be your job to care for the guinea pig.

A safe, well-equipped cage is a guinea pig necessity.

If you or someone in your family has allergies, will you be able to live with a guinea pig? Guinea pigs can cause severe allergic reactions in some people. Take everyone in your family to a pet store or guinea pig breeder to see if anyone has allergies to guinea pig dander. Find this out before you bring the guinea pig home.

If you love other animals besides guinea pigs, then you probably have another issue to think about: other pets. Do you have a dog or a cat? If you add a guinea pig to your home, you will need to think about how your other pets will act toward the newcomer, and how the inclusion of the guinea pig is going to affect their lives.

Guinea pigs are instinctively afraid of dogs, and rightfully so, since a dog can easily kill a guinea pig. Most dogs are aggressive toward rodents and will attack them. Cats, while not very dangerous to a rodent as large as an adult guinea pig, can also be less-than-friendly to guinea pigs.

Guinea pigs need a safe place to exercise in, free of household dangers like exposed electrical wires.

You will need to do a lot of work to either keep your guinea pig separated from your other animals or to somehow ensure that they all get along.

If your guinea pig is going to live in your house with you, then you must be willing to make changes in your environment. Guinea pigs are chewers, and homes that have guinea pigs must be chew-proofed. This requires considerable time and effort. And then there's always the chance that your guinea pig may outwit you and damage something valuable with those destructive teeth. Are you willing to face this possibility?

An important point that many people fail to consider is the legality of guinea pig ownership. Many ordinances do not allow pet rodents in residential areas.

Are you zoned for guinea pigs? This, of course, is best discovered before you bring home a new pet.

Another consideration is cost. The price of the guinea pig and her cage is just the beginning. After you bring your pet home, you will have to pay for food, possible spaying or neutering and vet bills should your guinea pig become ill.

But most important of all, are you willing to make an emotional commitment to your guinea pig? Are you prepared to accept responsibility for a living creature who is solely dependent on you for her well-being? Are you willing to make your pet's health and happiness a priority in your life? If your answer to these questions is yes, then you just might be ready to join the ranks of guinea pig owners everywhere.

The Joys of Owning a Guinea Pig

In the world of pet ownership, there are few things more rewarding than knowing that a guinea pig loves you and trusts you. This attitude on the part of your guinea pig is something that has to be earned, not bought. You can only establish this kind of rapport with your pet once you have spent time with her, showing her that you are worthy of her confidence.

Guinea pigs are prey animals (in the wild, they are food for larger predators) and this makes them suspicious by nature. How else would they survive? Because of this, they are often fearful and nervous. But once they learn that they are safe in their environment, the depth of their personality comes shining through.

Guinea pigs are not always thought of as intelligent creatures, but in reality, they are a lot smarter than most people think. They are bright animals with complex social structures who develop relationships with individual people and even animals of other species.

Life with a guinea pig means staying on your toes. They are active and inquisitive, and are always exploring their environments. Aside from being endearing, this kind of behavior can also get them into trouble. This is why guinea pig owners need to be especially vigilant about their pets' whereabouts at all times.

Many people find it surprising to know that guinea pigs can learn to recognize the sound of their favorite humans' voices. They can also learn that the opening of the refrigerator means a treat and the crackling of plastic means food is on its way. Many guinea pigs can be also be trained to do a variety of simple tricks. Some talented guinea pigs can learn to use a litter box.

Like all animals, guinea pigs have a body language that they use to communicate with members of their own species. Humans who learn to comprehend that language will better understand what their guinea pigs are telling them on a daily basis. Once there is this kind of understanding between human and guinea pig, the bond deepens.

People who live with guinea pigs soon discover that dogs and cats

> ### BENEFITS OF GUINEA PIG OWNERSHIP
>
> More and more people are discovering what makes guinea pigs such wonderful pets. Some of the things people like most about guinea pigs are:
>
> • they don't require long walks or bathroom breaks
>
> • they don't require a lot of room
>
> • they can be trained to use a litter box
>
> • they are entertaining and curious animals
>
> • they are social and can bond with their owners and other animals

have not cornered the market when it comes to love and affection. Guinea pigs can be very warm-hearted creatures. They adore being petted and love to fall asleep in the lap of a trusted person. Guinea pigs have a large capacity for affection and thrive when they receive love in return.

GUINEA PIGS AND CHILDREN

Children and guinea pigs can be great friends. Responsible children will even be able to take a large role in caring for the guinea pig. Although a parent should never expect the child to take ultimate responsibility for the guinea pig, allotting guinea pig chores is one way to let everyone in the family participate in the pet's life. Set reasonable goals for your child depending on his or her maturity. A younger child may help out by offering the guinea pig a treat (like fruit or green vegetables) every day, while an older child can be expected to feed the guinea pig and check her water supply daily. Whatever your child's responsibility, praise him or her for a job well done. You don't want to make the guinea pig a subject your child would rather avoid. And remember that you must take over your child's responsibilities even if he or she forgets them; otherwise, it is the helpless guinea pig who suffers in your struggle to teach your child responsibility.

In addition to helping care for the guinea pig, children can have fun with these pets. Your child can help construct toys for the guinea pig out of toilet paper tubes, paper bags, empty tissue boxes and other safe objects. Let your child use his or her imagination. Another fun guinea pig activity is simple observation. This is a good way to have your child learn about animal behavior in general and rodent behavior in particular. Another good way to get your child involved with his or her pet is to join a 4-H program. See chapter 10 for more information on this exciting hobby.

Younger children can also have a great deal of fun with a guinea pig, although they will need to be supervised. A guinea pig is a great way to teach them to respect other living things. Show them how to be gentle with their pet guinea pig. Let them pat the guinea pig on the floor, but don't allow them to pick her up. Young children can get startled or annoyed, or may just not be able to hold the guinea pig properly. As a result, the guinea pig may get dropped and injured. Instead, hold the guinea pig yourself and allow your child to pet her.

Your Children's Friends

Although your child may be mature enough to handle the guinea pig carefully and gently, you cannot be sure his or her friends will be. If your child wants to show off the pet to friends, make sure you are there to supervise the show and tell.

Finding a Guinea Pig

When it's time to embark on your journey to guinea pig ownership, you'll want to start out on the right foot by looking for your new companion in the best way possible.

ADOPTION

If you are simply looking for a pet guinea pig, one to share your life and be a companion, you should first consider adoption. Just as with dogs and cats, there are homeless guinea pigs in desperate need of loving families. Every day, unwanted guinea pigs are being put to sleep at animal shelters all over the country.

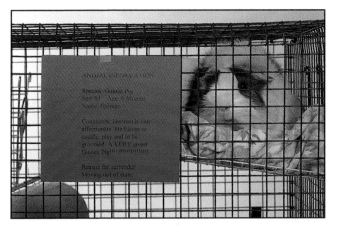

Guinea pigs who have been given up for adoption are usually victims of circumstance, and are capable of love and affection if given the chance.

Guinea pigs in need of adoption are usually hapless creatures who once belonged to a family. They may have been purchased impulsively or were the result of an unplanned litter. Through no fault of their own, they are later discarded. They deserve a second chance with a family who will love them and care for them throughout their lives.

If you would like to provide a home for a guinea pig who is desperately in need of one, there are several ways to go about it. First, call the animal shelters in your area and inquire about guinea pigs available for adoption. If you stop by the shelter in person and do not see any guinea pigs on display, be sure to ask if any are available, since many shelters keep guinea pigs in a back room away from the dogs and cats. Since unwanted guinea pigs are euthanized at shelters just like dogs and cats, adopting a guinea pig directly from a shelter means you will be saving a life.

You may also want to check the classified section of your local newspaper, as well as bulletin boards in supermarkets, veterinarians' offices and pet supply stores to see if there are people trying to find homes for guinea pigs in your area.

If you choose to adopt from someone who is working to find a new home for a guinea pig, the individual trying to place the guinea pig may ask you a lot of questions when you call. Any caring person who is trying to place a guinea pig in a new home has the responsibility to ask questions about the potential adoptive home to determine if the situation is right for both the guinea pig and the new owner.

You may also be asked to pay a small adoption fee. This is usually done for the purpose of weeding out unscrupulous people who may only be looking for a free guinea pig to feed to a pet reptile or to use for some other unsavory purpose. Adoption fees also help guinea pig rescuers offset the costs of caing for a homeless guinea pig until a new owner is found.

When conducting your adoption search, you will probably come across non-purebred guinea pigs in need of homes. There are mixed breed guinea pigs, just as there are mixed breed dogs. Consider bringing one of these guinea pigs into your life. Mixed breeds are often attractive guinea pigs and have an interesting quality that most purebreds don't: Each one is truly unique.

But if you have your heart set on a purebred guinea pig, there are also many purebred guinea pigs in need of good homes.

BUYING A GUINEA PIG

When considering the purchase of a guinea pig, it's important that you not make your acquisition impulsively. All pets need and deserve a certain level of commitment from their owners. Guinea pigs can live as long as seven years. The adorable baby guinea pig in the window may be tiny and cute now, but in a few months she will be a large adult needing consistent care. Impulse buying of pets often results in unhappiness for the owner and a sorry fate for the animal.

Breeders

If you have seriously considered whether or not you want to own a guinea pig and you plan to show your pet, purchasing is an important option. The best place to buy a guinea pig is from a responsible breeder. Responsible breeders are guinea pig fanciers who research bloodlines before breeding their guinea pigs and who keep their animals in clean and healthy environments. They are experts on their breed of choice, and frequently show their animals.

Baby guinea pigs are certainly adorable, but make sure you are prepared to care for the guinea pig as she grows into an adult.

Buying your pet from a responsible breeder will help to ensure that you are obtaining the breed of guinea pig that is best for you. There are different breeds of guinea pigs, all with their own special qualities. If you buy a young purebred guinea pig from a breeder, you will know exactly what she will look like when she matures. This method will also allow you to check on one or both of your pet's parents, giving you the opportunity to see what their

21

personalities are like since their offspring are likely to have similar temperaments. The breeder will also ask you questions to help both of you determine whether or not you are choosing the best breed for you.

A responsible breeder will welcome you, as a prospective buyer, into his or her breeding operation, allowing you to see firsthand the environment that the guinea pig has been living in. This way, you will be able to gauge whether or not your prospective pet has been well cared for and is living in clean and healthy conditions.

Buying from a breeder also offers an added bonus. Once you purchase your guinea pig, you go home with the name and phone number of an experienced contact who can answer your questions and provide you with help should you need it. If you are interested in showing your guinea pig, your breeder can help you get started in that area, too.

Once you have determined the breed you want, you can obtain the name and phone number of a breeder in your area by contacting one of the regional clubs in your area or by getting in touch with the American Cavy Breeders Association (see Chapter 12, "Resources").

Another way to find a guinea pig breeder is to attend a local rabbit and cavy show. Walk around and look at the different guinea pig breeds and speak to some of the exhibitors. Let people know you are looking for a breeder, and they will direct you to the appropriate individuals.

Your local 4-H group is another possible source for breeders. Call the local county extension office (listed in your telephone book) and ask for the name and number of a 4-H guinea pig leader in your area. This person should be able to put you in touch with a breeder nearby.

Pet Stores

Many people buy guinea pigs from pet stores. If you choose to purchase your pet from a retailer, make sure the store environment is clean and that the guinea pigs and other small animals are healthy and well-kept. Be sure to get a health guarantee on any animal you purchase.

Things to Consider When Choosing Your Guinea Pig

AGE

Age is not a very important factor when buying a guinea pig as long as the animal has been handled from a young age.

Adult guinea pigs can make wonderful pets. Since guinea pigs usually live anywhere from five to seven years, you can adopt or purchase a guinea pig that is several years old and still have a lot of time left to spend with her.

If your heart is set on getting a baby guinea pig, make sure the one you buy is at least four weeks old. Young guinea pigs should stay with their mothers until they are a month old. Taking them away too soon can be damaging both emotionally and physically, and guinea pigs removed from their mother's care too early rarely survive for long once they arrive in their new home.

HEALTH

It's important to start out on the right foot by selecting a guinea pig who is in good health. A guinea pig's general health can be determined in a number of ways. Check to see if her ears and nose are clean and free of discharge and debris. Then, take a close look at her fur. The fur of a healthy guinea pig will be soft, shiny and even. Keep an eye out for lice in the ears and fur, bald spots and signs of diarrhea.

Feel the guinea pig's body. It should be round, tight and smooth. However if the abdomen is hard and round, the guinea pig may be suffering from a worm infestation.

23

Attitude is also important when determining a guinea pig's health. Look for an animal who is bright-eyed, alert and active. A guinea pig who appears dull and listless is probably sick.

Be sure to take notice of the guinea pig's surroundings. Are they clean and relatively odor-free? Are the animals kept in spacious, airy cages? Do the other guinea pigs appear healthy? Many guinea pig diseases are contagious. If the guinea pig you are considering for purchase is housed near a sick guinea pig, chances are that your pet will come down with the same illness.

A healthy guinea pig has soft, shiny fur, a round, firm body and an alert expression.

Look at the guinea pig's teeth and determine whether or not the two top teeth overlap the two lower teeth. Do not buy a guinea pig whose teeth do not fit this description unless you are prepared to have the teeth trimmed regularly by a veterinarian. A condition called malocclusion, in which the upper incisors do not overlap the lower incisors, is a serious problem in guinea pigs and can result in much grief to both guinea pig and owner if not properly managed. Misaligned teeth do not wear down properly and can grow out of control. Unless they are clipped regularly by a veterinarian, they will cause mouth infections and jaw problems, and can even grow so long, that they will curve back into the guinea pig's skull and kill the animal.

Check around the cage to make sure that the guinea pig's fecal pellets are round and hard. Diarrhea is a sign of illness.

If you are buying your pet from a breeder, talk to him or her about the guinea pig you are interested in. Ask questions about the animal's ancestors. What were their personalities like? Did they have any health problems that could be genetic? If you plan to show your guinea pig, ask about the show careers of the guinea pig's parents and grandparents. Ask to see the guinea pig's sire (father) and dam (mother). Study the standard for the breed that you are considering and try to apply it to the guinea pig's parents. If they are good specimens of the breed, chances are that their off-spring will be, too.

While you are discussing the guinea pig with the breeder or retailer, ask him or her if they have a return policy should the guinea pig become ill. If you have other pets, particularly a dog, you should also find out if the seller will take the guinea pig back if your other pets will not accept her into the household.

PERSONALITY

If you give your guinea pig love and attention, chances are she will become a wonderful pet. However, when you are selecting your guinea pig, you may want to observe the personality of the animals you are considering to see which one strikes your fancy. Guinea pigs who appear nervous and afraid may be high-strung, or just unused to being handled. If

Check to make sure your guinea pig's front teeth overlap the lower ones. Misaligned teeth can cause lots of problems.

the animal is young, she is still very impressionable and will learn to be held and stroked if you show her love and consideration. Older guinea pigs who have not been handled much will need more work to make them comfortable with people. Eventually, they should learn to respond to care and affection.

GENDER

There is some debate in guinea pig circles over which make better pets: males or females. The answer really depends on what you plan to do with your pet.

Females (sows) are said to be mainly concerned with reproducing. They emit an odor and are very interested in breeding with males that they meet.

Males (boars), on the other hand, are thought to be somewhat aggressive and unsettled. They also have a strong odor and will be territorial with other males.

If you plan to purchase two guinea pigs who will live together in the same cage, make sure that you receive accurate information about the animals' gender. Male and female guinea pigs can be hard tell apart, especially when they are young. Get expert advice from a breeder or veterinarian about the gender of your pets before you place them together.

Spaying and Neutering

Worries about gender and reproduction can be solved very simply—by spaying and neutering. Pet guinea pigs who will not be shown or bred should be spayed or neutered. Once this is done, their troublesome hormones will disappear, they will be healthier and you will have a gentler, loving pet. Preventing your pet from having a litter will also help curb the guinea pig overpopulation problem, meaning fewer guinea pigs in animal shelters being put to sleep.

If you decide to spay or neuter your guinea pig, then gender should not be a factor in your purchasing decision, since spayed sows and neutered boars make equally good pets. Remember, though, that if you plan to have more than one guinea pig and you do not want to spay or neuter your pets, you will need to get two females, since two unneutered males will fight with one another.

PEDIGREE

If you are purchasing a purebred guinea pig from a breeder, ask the breeder for a signed pedigree paper. This document will state your guinea pig's sex, color and parentage. You may later choose to register your guinea pig with the American Rabbit Breeders

Association if you want to show the animal at local guinea pig shows.

Naming Your Guinea Pig

Once you choose your guinea pig, you will need to name her. If you have children, allow them to participate in choosing the name. You can get inspiration from the guinea pig's color ("Blackie") or shape ("Peanut"), or personality ("Lucky"). Whatever you do, don't chose something that's funny or unkind. You will be using your guinea pig's name for years to come, so make sure that it's an attractive name that bears repeating.

chapter 3

Breeds

of **Guinea Pigs**

In nature, there is just one type and color of guinea pig. However, over the years breeders have produced many beautiful varieties of guinea pig from that single wild strain. But how did this happen? How did the tremendous variety that now exists develop from one type of guinea pig?

Basic Genetics

This is not the time or place to go into a detailed discussion of genetics, but a general overview will help you to understand how new guinea pig varieties are produced.

28

A large degree of genetic diversity exists in every animal that reproduces sexually. This genetic diversity enables a species to adapt to changes in its environment, making the species better able to survive in a shifting world. In a vastly simplified explanation, a guinea pig inherits two genes for a specific trait, coat color for example, one from his father and one from his mother. Each of the genes is either dominant or recessive, and the color of the guinea pig's coat depends on which of the two genes is dominant.

When some guinea pigs became domesticated, however, human beings could control which they were breeding. When an unusual trait showed up in a guinea pig, this animal was consciously bred with another guinea pig who had a similar trait. In this way, the unusual trait turned up in the guinea pigs' offspring, rather than being lost again, perhaps forever, as it would have been if the unusual guinea pig was mated with a normal guinea pig. In this way, guinea pig breeders have been able to produce the many beautiful colors and varieties included in this chapter. And new and amazing varieties are still being developed.

Underneath the fancy coat of a purebred guinea pig, however, he is the same as any other guinea pig and needs your affection and care.

Guinea Pig Colors

Guinea pigs come in a number of colors, each with his own unique beauty. Guinea pig colors are arranged in groups. Within each group, there are individual colors. Below are general definitions of each color group.

Agouti Pattern The hair shaft of an agouti-colored guinea pig has several bands of color. Two or more alternating light or dark rings determine the color of agouti. The eyes must be a specific color associated with the individual agouti color. Wild guinea pigs show the original agouti coloring.

Marked Pattern Guinea pigs with the marked pattern are usually white with patterns of another color throughout their bodies.

*A self-pattern
chocolate
guinea pig.*

Self Pattern   This term is used to describe solid-colored guinea pigs, those who have a uniform color throughout the entire body.

Solid Pattern   This is similar to the self pattern, except that it may include agouti and other mixed-color fur as long as this fur does not create a pattern or marking.

While each breed has its own breed standard and selection of color varieties, there are common colors that can be found in many different breeds. Following are descriptions of some of the most common guinea pig colors.

Beige   Guinea pigs of this color have a beige pigment throughout their bodies, including their ears and feet. Their eyes are pink.

Black   In guinea pigs, black is a deep, rich color that goes all the way to the skin, with matching ears and feet. The eyes are also black.

Blue   Blue coloration can be described as a medium shade of gray with a blue or lavender cast. The eyes of a blue guinea pig are dark blue.

Brindle   Brindle, a color also seen commonly in dogs, is an intermingling of red and black hairs. The brindle pattern appears consistently throughout the body, and the eyes are dark.

Broken Color This is more of a marking than a color. Broken-color guinea pigs have coats bearing clean-cut patches of two or more recognized colors. Exceptions are the tortoise shell, Himalayan, tortoise shell and white, Dalmatian and Dutch colorations.

Chocolate A deep, dark brown, the coloration of a chocolate guinea pig is carried all the way to the skin. The eyes are brown or dark brown with a red cast.

Cream This is a delicate off-white that is even all over. The eyes of a cream guinea pig are red or dark.

Dalmatian Just like the dog of the same name, Dalmatian guinea pigs have a coat with dark spots over a white background. The spots can be in the colors of beige, black, blue, chocolate, cream, lilac, orange or red.

Dutch guinea pig.

Dutch The markings of the Dutch-colored guinea pig consist of a dark coloration on the chest, neck, forelegs and face, in combination with white. The markings are clear and distinct.

Golden Agouti Guinea pigs of this color are a chestnut color with an undercoat of blue-black. The coat should also have black ticking. The eyes are dark.

Himalayan The body color of a Himalayan-colored guinea pig is white, with black markings on the nose, feet and ears. The eyes are pink.

Lilac This coloration features a medium gray hue with a purplish tint over the guinea pig's entire body, ears and feet. The eyes are pink or dark with a ruby cast.

Red Red guinea pigs are a deep, rich red, with matching ears and feet. The eyes are dark.

Red-Eyed Orange As the name implies, guinea pigs of this coloration are a reddish-orange color with a ruby-red eye.

Roan This coloration consists of white hairs mixed with one or two other colors. The eyes and ears match the corresponding hair color that is mixed with white.

Silver Agouti Guinea pigs of this color are a bright silver-white, which is caused by a blue-black undercoat tipped with white. Silver agouti guinea pigs have dark eyes with a reddish cast.

Tortoise Shell Guinea pigs with this coloration sport patches of red hair and patches of black hair, which make up a checkerboard pattern over their bodies. Tortoise shell guinea pigs have dark eyes.

Tortoise Shell and White Tortoise shell and white guinea pigs have patches of red, black and white hair that alternate from one side of the animal to the other. Their eyes are dark.

White In guinea pigs, this coloration is a pure white with no brassy or yellow tinge. The eyes are either pink or a dark color.

Popular Breeds

There are twelve breeds of domesticated guinea pigs recognized by the American Rabbit Breeders Association, the official registry for guinea pigs in the United States. Each breed is a wonder in and of itself, differing in color, body type and coat from all the others. Some have short, round bodies. Others have longer, more streamlined figures. Coat color, markings and coat texture are unique in each breed. Each of these breeds is available in the agouti, self, solid and marked varieties.

When determining which breed to acquire, keep your needs and lifestyle in mind. If your time is limited, you'll definitely want to stay away from the long-haired breeds since they require frequent grooming.

Narrow your choice down to a few breeds, and then find the one that appeals to you the most. You might want to attend a guinea pig show in your area to see a number of the breeds up close. This will allow you to compare their colors, coat lengths and general appearance. In the end, you should choose a breed that fits your lifestyle and appeals to you aesthetically.

Abyssinian.

Abyssinian The Abyssinian guinea pig is one of the oldest breeds, and has a unique appearance. His coat is covered with rosettes, a pattern made up of radiated hair growing from a center point. The rosettes are placed one on each shoulder, four over the back, one on each hip and two across the guinea pig's rear. The coat of the Abyssinian is coarse and dense, and measures around 1 $^1/_2$ inches in length. The Abyssinian has a medium body length with rounded sides, and plenty of depth to the shoulders and hindquarters.

Abyssinian Satin.

Abyssinian Satin The Abyssinian Satin has a shiny coat as his name suggests. He is covered with rosettes exactly like those of the Abyssinian.

American   The American is the most popular breed of guinea pig, and has the appearance that most people think of when they imagine a typical guinea pig. He has a Roman, or rounded, nose with ears that stick out of the sides of his head. His smooth coat lies close to his body.

American.

American Satin   The American Satin is the same as the American guinea pig, except that his coat is shiny and sleek.

American Satin.

Peruvian   The Peruvian guinea pig used to be known as the Angora. This breed sports a long, sweeping coat that drags on the ground. The Peruvian's hair, which grows from a center part down the animal's back, is very dense and soft, and requires a lot of grooming. Peruvian guinea pigs do best if their long hair is trimmed back for ease in grooming and so the animal can see where he is going.

Peruvian Satin   The Peruvian Satin is very similar to the Peruvian except that his coat is much silkier and more lustrous.

Peruvian.

Silkie   The Silkie guinea pig, known as the Sheltie in England, is so named because of the softness of his very long hair. The hair grows back from the guinea pig's nose and over his back in a teardrop pattern. Because of his luxurious coat, the Silkie also requires a lot of grooming.

Silkie.

Silkie Satin   The only difference between the Silkie and the Silkie Satin is the coat. The Silkie Satin's hair is very long, dense and lustrous like the Silkie's, but it has a distinctive sheen.

35

Teddy   The Teddy guinea pig was created from a mutation. The breed has a dense, resilient, kinky coat that is about ³/₄ inch in length. Two different textures are seen in the Teddy's coat: plush, which is soft, and harsh, which is rough.

Teddy.

Teddy Satin   Like the Teddy, the Teddy Satin has a short, dense and kinky coat, although it will reveal a glowing sheen in the right lighting.

Teddy Satin.

White Crested   The White Crested is set apart from the other guinea pig breeds by a single white rosette that sits atop his head. This marking is very difficult to breed for, and consequently, there are not many show-quality White Cresteds alive today. A correct crest is centered on a line running from the tip of the guinea pig's nose to the center of his ears. In a show-quality White Crested, there are no other white hairs on the body.

White Crested.

Coronet The Coronet is the newest breed of guinea pig recognized by the American Rabbit Breeders Association. The Coronet sports a long coat with a large rosette—or coronet—that runs from the tip of the nose to the center of the ears. The ears droop slightly.

Caring
for Your

part two

Guinea Pig

4

Bringing Your
Guinea Pig
Home

You've chosen the guinea pig that you are going to adopt or purchase. Before you bring her home, you will need to prepare her environment. Shopping for and setting up all the equipment and supplies you'll need for your guinea pig before her arrival will make her introduction to your home less stressful for both of you.

What You'll Need

The first and most important item to purchase will be your guinea pig's cage. If you are buying an outdoor cage, or hutch, this will be your most significant financial investment. Take your time finding the one that best suits your needs or build it yourself. Leave yourself plenty of time to construct the hutch before its inhabitant arrives.

(See Chapter 6, "Outdoor Guinea Pigs," for information on how to buy a hutch.)

If you are buying an indoor guinea pig cage, it is best to get it before your pet comes home so it will be set up and ready to accommodate her. (See Chapter 5, "Indoor Guinea Pigs," for information on how to select an indoor cage.)

Create a comfortable home for your guinea pig before she arrives so she can settle in right away.

You should also purchase or create a nest box for your guinea pig. This will help her feel more secure. (See Chapter 5, "Indoor Guinea Pigs," for information on nest boxes.)

AMENITIES

Your guinea pig will need more than just a cage to live a comfortable and healthy life. There are a number of cage accessories that you should purchase before her arrival.

Your guinea pig's food bowl is very important, and should be chosen wisely. Don't use any old dish you have in the cupboard, as guinea pigs will chew up or knock over the wrong kind of food container. Instead, take a trip to your local pet supply store and buy a ceramic crock made specifically for pets. Ceramic crocks are chew resistant and difficult to knock over.

When you purchase a food crock, keep your guinea pig's size in mind. Don't buy a dish that's too small for the guinea pig to put her head into, or too big for her to reach into comfortably.

Another option is a metal bowl that attaches to the side of the cage. When selecting a metal bowl, be sure that it's not so deep that the guinea pig can't reach all the way into it. Make sure the bowl is attached to the side of the cage at a low enough level to allow easy access.

Another necessity for your guinea pig's cage is a water bottle. Gravity water bottles are readily available in pet supply stores. These are the best type of water containers for guinea pigs since they are impossible to knock over. The water stays clean in a water bottle because the guinea pig is unable to drop food into it or otherwise soil it.

When you purchase a water bottle for your guinea pig's cage, make sure it is not too small. You want your guinea pig to drink as much water as possible to maintain her health, and a small bottle will need filling more than once a day.

Also, make sure the water bottle you purchase has a metal ball inserted into the tip. This will keep it from leaking in your guinea pig's cage.

A hay rack is another important item for the

Some of the supplies you'll need for your guinea pig include a cage, grooming equipment, toys and food.

cage. Hay is a vital element in your guinea pig's daily diet. A hay rack will hold the hay in place so it doesn't get scattered throughout the cage. Hay racks are usually made of metal, and will attach to the upper side of the cage. The guinea pig can pull strands of hay from the rack whenever she gets the urge to munch.

A supply of food should be on hand. Find out what your guinea pig has been eating in her previous home and begin by offering her these same items. If you need to change her diet, you'll have to do so over a period of a few weeks so as not to upset her digestion. (See Chapter 7, "Nutrition and Grooming," for information on what to feed your guinea pig.)

You'll need a litter box and litter if you are planning to try to litter box train your guinea pig. A small litter box made for a cat can be good for a guinea pig, providing the box is not too large. (See Chapter 5, "Indoor Guinea Pigs," for complete information about litter box training your guinea pig.)

You'll want to have bedding available for your guinea pig as well. Guinea pigs enjoy sleeping on wood shavings, shredded paper, processed ground corn cob and commercial bedding pellets. Wood shavings, shredded paper, corn cob and bedding

Use a water bottle with a metal ball in the tip to provide your guinea pig with a constant supply of fresh water.

pellets made especially for small animals can be purchased in any pet supply shop. (Some experts believe that cedar shavings can be detrimental to a guinea pig's respiratory system. While there is no scientific evidence to confirm this, many guinea pig owners prefer to use other, less aromatic, bedding for their pets.)

Since guinea pigs are gnawing mammals, you'll need to have something safe and chewable in your guinea pig's cage in the form of chewing blocks. Untreated wood can be used, but the safest items to give your guinea pig to gnaw on are commercially prepared wood blocks or chews, obtainable from pet supply stores. Available in a variety of colors and shapes, these gnawing treats are made especially for animals that chew, and are safe and inexpensive.

Many people are surprised to learn that guinea pigs love to play with toys. A toy for a guinea pig can be anything from an empty toilet paper roll to a small cardboard box. Having a few items on hand when your guinea pig arrives will help her feel at home in her new environment. While she might not play with these items right away, she will appreciate their presence once she becomes acclimated to her new environment.

Guinea pigs appreciate toys of all kinds.

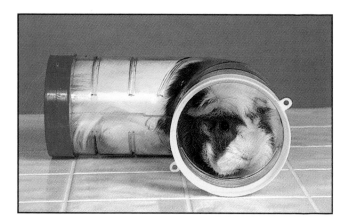

Additional Items

Besides the previously mentioned cage accessories, there are a few other articles you'll want to have on hand before you bring your guinea pig home.

First and foremost is a travel carrier. You should purchase one before your guinea pig makes the trip home with you, since you may need to use it for the journey. A small, plastic, airline-approved carrier works best for guinea pigs. Make sure you line the carrier bottom with newspaper so the guinea pig won't slide around during the car ride home.

Your carrier will come in handy for trips to the vet and for confining your guinea pig whenever you clean her cage or need to keep her temporarily in a small space. A good carrier is a wise investment.

Since guinea pigs need regular grooming, a brush or comb should be on your shopping list. A slicker or pin brush is best for brushing guinea pigs' fur. This type of brush is gentle yet effective at removing snarls and mats.

If your guinea pig is a shorthaired breed, then a flea comb (the type used for cats) is a good combing tool. If your guinea pig is of a longhaired variety, then you'll need a wide-toothed comb rather than a fine-toothed flea comb.

Since a guinea pig's toenails need to be trimmed regularly, make sure you have a nail trimmer. The guillotine-type used for cutting cats' nails will work, although many guinea pig owners prefer to use human nail clippers instead.

Acclimating the Newcomer

When your new guinea pig comes into your home for the first time, it will be an exciting moment. Everyone in the family will be anxious to feel her soft fur and watch her investigate her new environment.

As exhilarating as this moment will be, it is important to realize that your guinea pig will have a different perspective on the situation. Put yourself in her place for a moment: She's just been taken from her familiar surroundings, stuck in a box and whisked away to a place she's never seen. Everything is new to her. There's little doubt she will be overwhelmed.

Because of the guinea pig's innate need to always be alert for predators, you may notice that your new pet seems skittish and fearful in her new environment. Remember that this is normal guinea pig behavior. Your pet will need a lot of love, patience and understanding to learn to relax. Be sure to give her a place to hide when she is being introduced to her new situation. This will provide her with much-needed security.

NECESSARY SUPPLIES

Make a trip to the pet supply store so you'll have the necessary items on hand before you bring your guinea pig home. This way she'll settle in and get used to her hew surroundings as quickly as possible.

- cage
- food bowl
- hay rack
- water bottle with metal tip
- food supply
- chewing blocks
- toys

The kindest way to let your guinea pig get used to her new home is to leave her alone for awhile. Place her in her cage—which you equipped with food, water and everything she'll need to survive—and then let her check things out in privacy for a couple of hours.

After your guinea pig has had a chance to get used to her new cage, you can begin to quietly observe her. Speak to her softly every so often to reassure her that everything is okay and to let her get accustomed to your voice.

If you have children, this is a good time to start teaching them how to treat their new guinea pig. Explain to them that their new pet needs peace and quiet so she can learn to feel comfortable in her new home.

Hold your guinea pig with one hand under her forelegs, the other one supporting her rear.

If your children are anxious to show their new guinea pig to their friends, ask their friends to come in to visit one or two at a time so they don't scare the animal. They should be as quiet as possible when they are near the new pet. Guinea pigs' ears are very sensitive, and loud noises can be frightening.

Be sure that your children understand that they should not handle the guinea pig right away. Because the new guinea pig will be fearful and skittish, any attempts to hold her may result in injury to the guinea pig. It's vital that you first learn the proper way to handle a guinea pig, and then teach your child to do so. Once your child has learned handling techniques, always supervise the handling to make sure it is being done correctly. A guinea pig's skeleton is fragile, and dropping a squirming guinea pig to the ground could result in fatal injury.

It's also important to keep other pets away from the new guinea pig while she is getting used to her surroundings. Your guinea pig needs time to adjust to her new life, and it is best to introduce her to each element one step at a time. At first, keep her cage in an area that is somewhat secluded, where cats and dogs can't bother her. Later, when she is feeling more comfortable, you can have her meet your other pets. (See page 48 for information on how to introduce your guinea pig to your cat or dog.)

Handling Your Guinea Pig

Guinea pigs do not like to be lifted and held unless they are gradually taught to tolerate it. If your guinea pig has not been held very much in her life, it will require skill and patience to teach her to accept it.

Since guinea pigs are not natural climbers, your pet will feel awkward and insecure when lifted off the ground. As a result, she may struggle frantically. A fall can seriously injure a guinea pig. For this reason, you must learn to hold your guinea pig properly and securely.

Never, ever lift a guinea pig by any of her limbs. This practice is dangerous and painful to the guinea pig. Also, be careful never to hold a guinea pig tightly by her midsection. A tight grip on this area of the body could result in internal injuries.

Before you begin practicing picking up and carrying your guinea pig, be sure to wear protective clothing. Bare skin and unclipped guinea pig nails don't mix!

The best way to pick up a guinea pig is to place one hand underneath the animal so that the legs are on either side of your hand, and then lift her, using the other hand to hold up her rear. Holding the animal against your chest in this manner helps her feel secure.

If the guinea pig begins to struggle during the handling process, bend down to your knees. This will keep her from falling too far should you lose your grip on her.

If you have children, you should keep a close eye on them when they wish to handle the guinea pig. Teach them the proper way to lift and carry a guinea pig, and always supervise them when they are doing so. Because guinea pigs are fragile, and incorrect handling can result in a severely injured animal, very small children should not be permitted to pick up or carry a guinea pig. Petting a guinea pig while she has all four feet safely on the floor is a better approach when very young children are involved.

Teach your children the proper way to hold the guinea pig, but remember that patting a guinea pig with all four feet on the ground is usually the safest option.

Remember when handling your guinea pig to always treat her gently and carefully. Since being lifted and carried are not natural for a guinea pig, you will need patience and kindness to help your new pet accept this type of handling.

Introducing Other Pets

Guinea pigs are very social animals. In the wild, they live in large groups and have a complex social hierarchy. They therefore can get along famously with other pets, including cats, dogs, rabbits and other guinea pigs. However, whether or not there is harmony in a particular multi-pet household depends largely on the individual animals involved, as well as the owner.

If your guinea pig is going to live happily in your house, she will need to get used to your other pets. It can take considerable time, patience and commitment to teach your dog or cat to get along with a new guinea pig. Never force pets on each other, and always supervise your animals while they are together. Make sure that you devote special attention to this aspect of guinea pig ownership since your guinea pig's existence depends on it.

GUINEA PIGS AND DOGS

When it comes to dogs, guinea pig owners have to take special care. Dogs and guinea pigs are natural enemies—dogs are predators and guinea pigs are prey animals. It is instinctive for dogs to chase and kill guinea pigs, and it's instinctive for guinea pigs to fear dogs and run from them. If you are going to keep both a guinea pig and a dog as pets, you need to be aware of this inherent tension between the two creatures.

The safest way to handle a dog-guinea pig relationship is to never allow the dog and guinea pig to be loose together in the home or backyard. No dog can be completely trusted with a small rodent like a guinea pig. A dog can kill a guinea pig in a matter of seconds.

Most dogs can be trained to respect a caged guinea pig, however. They can be taught not to harass the guinea pig while she is in her cage and to leave you alone while you are holding your guinea pig in your arms.

If you already have a dog and would like to bring a guinea pig into your home, there are some points you should consider. First of all, think about your dog's personality. Is he a mellow old couch potato who is hard-pressed to get upset or excited? Or is he a younger, more active dog? Dogs that are older and calmer usually do better when new pets are introduced. Be careful, though. The mellowest of dogs can suddenly come to life when he sees a guinea pig scurrying across the floor.

If you do have a young, easily excitable dog, guinea pig ownership may still work out for you, provided you are able to control your dog. During the introduction process, you will have to be able to contain your dog's enthusiasm. If he ignores you when you call him and

49

basically marches to the beat of his own drummer, you will have a problem.

Assuming that your dog is controllable, think about his past relationships with other animals. Is he aggressive towards cats? Does he like to chase rabbits and other small animals around the yard or when you take him for a walk? Have you given him encouragement to do this? If your answer to these questions is yes, you will have a difficult time teaching your dog that the new guinea pig is hands-off, since he has already learned that it's okay to chase smaller animals. You can certainly give it a try, but you may have to consider keeping the two animals apart indefinitely or simply passing on guinea pig ownership.

Consider your dog's breed as well. Many terriers, some types of hounds and a number of other breeds have been bred for hundreds of years to hunt small mammals. If your dog comes from one of these hunting breeds, keep in mind that one look at your new guinea pig could trigger previously dormant hunting instincts in your dog. In this situation, you will have to work even harder to teach your dog to override his natural instincts and not harass your guinea pig.

If you have determined that your dog is controlled enough to attempt making friends with a guinea pig, you can begin the gradual process of introducing the two animals.

Make sure your new guinea pig has had some time to get used to her new home before you introduce her to your dog. Once she seems comfortable, start the proceedings by placing your dog on a leash and asking an adult whom the dog respects to be in control of him.

Allow your dog to gradually approach the guinea pig's cage in a quiet manner. If the dog gets rambunctious, correct him by saying "No!" and quickly jerking the leash. When the dog stands quietly, praise him to let him know that this is the kind of behavior you expect from him when he is close to the guinea pig.

When your guinea pig first lays eyes on your dog, she will undoubtedly be frightened. She will probably dive into her nest box and hide. Let her stay there, since she will feel much more secure this way. Eventually, if the dog behaves in a nonthreatening manner, the guinea pig may become braver and more curious, finally venturing out of the nest box to investigate.

Once the dog and guinea pig are comfortable with each other in this scenario and your guinea pig is used to being out of her cage without the dog present, you can try carrying your guinea pig in your arms with the dog present. Begin your session indoors by placing the dog on a leash. You may also want to muzzle him, just to be safe.

Take your guinea pig out of the cage and hold her in your arms as you move slowly across the room. Reassure the guinea pig with a soothing voice while the person holding the leash allows the dog to watch you. If the dog acts aggressively, correct him by saying "No" and jerking on the leash. If he sits by and quietly watches, praise him.

The guinea pig may become frightened by the dog's close proximity and the fact that she is outside of her cage, and may struggle to get away. Your dog's first impulse will be to get excited about this. Teach him that this is not acceptable, and don't allow him to run up and jump on you. Using the dog's obedience training, tell him to sit so that he will come to understand that this is a special animal that cannot be harmed in any way.

Repeat these scenarios until your dog gets the message. (Muzzling your dog while the guinea pig is in your arms is highly recommended until you are completely confident that he will not harm the guinea pig.) It may take a couple of months, but if you are consistent, you should see results.

GUINEA PIGS AND CATS

Cats are usually better companions for guinea pigs than dogs, primarily because the two species are more similar in size. While cats are predators and often inclined to chase guinea pigs, they are less capable of doing damage than dogs, which can kill a guinea pig with one snap of their jaws. It is rare that a cat will be so aggressive toward a guinea pig that the two cannot be housemates.

When preparing to introduce your cat and your guinea pig, start out by buying a harness for your cat and getting him used to wearing it. Having your cat wear the harness during the no-cage introduction will give you control over him should he become combative. You should also have a water-filled squirt gun handy in case your cat gets out of hand and you need to spray the cat to discipline him.

Start out by showing the guinea pig to your cat while the guinea pig is still in her cage. The two animals will be very wary of each other at first, and the guinea pig may hide in her nest box.

If your cat approaches tentatively and does not behave aggressively toward the guinea pig, reward him with praise and possibly even a treat. If he hisses at the guinea pig and runs away, ignore it. She will undoubtedly come back to investigate and will eventually get used to the intruder. If the cat reaches his arm into the cage and tries to get at the guinea pig, squirt the cat with the water pistol from a distance. This will let him know that aggressive behavior toward the guinea pig is not acceptable.

Once the two animals begin to ignore each other, you'll know that you are ready for the next step. Allow your guinea pig out of her cage indoors, with your cat on the harness. When the guinea pig moves, the cat may act as if he wants to chase her. Don't allow it. Instead, keep the cat still and let him watch the guinea pig move around the room until he gets used to the idea that he's not allowed to chase.

You will need to repeat these get-acquainted sessions on a regular basis until both animals are comfortable with each other. It may take some time, but in most cases, your efforts will pay off.

Of course, the safest way to have a cat and a guinea pig in the same home is to keep the guinea pig caged or secure in your arms while the cat is present. Never, under any circumstances, leave your cat and guinea pig alone together unsupervised.

OTHER GUINEA PIGS

Fostering cohabitation between two guinea pigs can be even more complicated than encouraging it among a dog and cat. In the wild, guinea pigs live with their own kind in complex societies. Whenever a guinea pig is introduced to a member of her own species, the two rodents have to figure out just where each one of them fits in the pecking order.

The first step toward a successful friendship among guinea pigs is spaying and neutering, particularly in the case of two males. Raging hormones can cause an intact male guinea pig to fight with another guinea pig he might normally get along with. Spaying and neutering both female and male guinea pigs eliminates hormones from the equation, making the animals calmer and more docile.

When deciding whether or not two guinea pigs will become friends, keep in mind that gender can be an important factor. Spayed females and neutered males tend to get along better than other gender combinations, although two intact females have been known to become good friends.

Introducing two guinea pigs is different than introducing a dog and a guinea pig or a cat and a guinea pig. Guinea pigs see other guinea pigs differently than they do members of others species and are capable of behaving much more aggressively with each other.

Neutered guinea pigs should become fast friends if you introduce them properly.

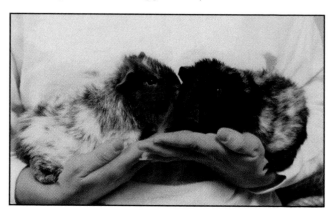

In many situations, guinea pigs who are strangers will behave assertively toward each other. This is why it is necessary to gradually allow them to get used to one another.

Begin by finding a place of neutral territory, where neither guinea pig has had a chance to stake a claim. This can be a room in the house where neither has ever been, or even the back seat of a parked car. Placing the guinea pigs on unclaimed turf will temper their instinctive urge to defend territory.

Keep the guinea pigs in their individual cages at first, and put the cages next to each other on neutral turf. Leave them together like this as often as possible.

Once their tensions have subsided and they seem less hostile toward each other through the bars of their cages, take them out and let them get close to each other in the neutral space. There might be some fighting, but you can break it up by squirting your water gun at the two culprits. Provided you have not mixed two intact males, the guinea pigs will eventually work things out and will learn to tolerate each other or, hopefully, become fast friends. Again, this is the most likely scenario if the guinea pigs are spayed or neutered.

Keep in mind that placing intact male and female guinea pigs together will soon result in numerous litters of baby guinea pigs. Since there are already more guinea pigs than there are homes for them, the most responsible thing to do is to avoid keeping males and females together. This problem of reproduction can be solved, or course, by having one or both animals spayed or neutered.

chapter 5

Indoor

Guinea Pigs

It's impossible to truly appreciate life with a guinea pig unless you keep him inside your home. Just like a dog or a cat, guinea pigs are companion animals with personalities all their own. If you don't actually live with a guinea pig, day in and day out, you'll never get to know him as well as you could. Likewise, the guinea pig won't get to know you that well.

If your guinea pig is outside most of the time, the two of you will lead separate lives. You will miss out on the chance to have him sleep on your lap while you watch TV and gaze up at you from the floor while you eat your dinner. People who live with indoor guinea pigs enjoy these antics and more from their pets.

There are also many other practical reasons for keeping a guinea pig indoors. Guinea pigs who live inside tend to live longer than outdoor guinea pigs. Bad weather and predators are responsible for the demise of many outdoor guinea pigs. These are consequences of outdoor living that even conscientious owners cannot always control.

Illness is a major cause of death among outdoor guinea pigs, mostly because outdoor pets are more difficult to monitor. Signs of sickness can be subtle at first, and since outdoor guinea pigs spend less time with their owners, it can be a day or so before the owner recognizes the illness. In the case of rapidly progressive illnesses, a delay of even one day can cost a guinea pig his life.

The decision to keep your guinea pig indoors is a wise one. Even guinea pigs who have been living outside for years can acclimate to a life indoors.

Indoor Housing

Even though your indoor guinea pig will have a roof over his head in a literal sense, he'll still need his own private retreat. A cage will offer security for your guinea pig, and can also offer him privacy and a safe haven.

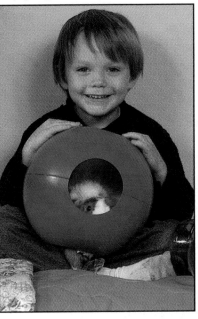

An indoor guinea pig will be able to enjoy family life.

Indoor guinea pig cages are readily available in pet supply stores and through catalogs, and there are a wide variety of styles. When searching for the right cage, look for one made from sturdy wire, with a removable bottom tray. Your guinea pig will not gnaw on the wire, and the removable tray will make cleaning easier. Wire will also allow your pet to receive the ventilation and light he needs.

A wire bottom or solid rustproof metal or hard plastic floor is suitable for a guinea pig. While a wire mesh bottom can make cage cleaning easier, it is not very safe for your guinea pig since his legs can easily get caught in it. Also, wire floors can result in sore feet and hocks. If you choose a wire floor, a solid area made of wood (any type except redwood, which is toxic) must be provided somewhere in the cage so the guinea pig can find relief from the wire bottom.

Indoor guinea pigs are safe from predators and protected from the weather.

Your indoor cage should be big enough for the guinea pig to stretch out and move around in while also accommodating a nest box, food and water accessories and a toy or two. The height of the cage should allow the guinea pig to stand up on his hind legs without his head touching the top.

Look for a cage that is well constructed and easy to disassemble for cleaning. It should also have a door on top so you will be able to reach inside, and a door on the side so the guinea pig can go in and out of the cage when he wishes.

NEST BOXES

Guinea pigs are burrowing animals by nature. In the wild, they live under the ground in dens they have dug. These burrows provide them with a sense of security. For this reason, guinea pigs who live above ground as pets enjoy having nest boxes, a substitute for burrows, inside their cages.

A nest box is a small boxlike enclosure that contains the animal's bedding and has an entry hole cut into it. It provides a safe place to sleep and hide. A cardboard box would work well as a nest box, but most guinea pigs will chew it to pieces, so wood is preferred.

Commercially made nest boxes are available through pet supply outlets and mail-order catalogs that specialize in small-animal supplies. Or, you can build your own.

Your guinea pig's nest box should be big enough for the animal to turn around in while several inches of bedding are in place. Make sure the entrance to the nest box is big enough for your guinea pig to gain entry, and that one side of the box is removable so you can clean it. There should be no sharp edges anywhere on the box.

LOCATION

When determining where in the house to place your guinea pig's cage, remember that extreme temperatures are dangerous for the animal. Do not put your guinea pig's cage in a spot where the sun will shine directly on it. Avoid keeping it near a radiator, stove, fireplace or other heating element.

Keep your guinea pig's cage in a frequently used part of the house, off the floor and out of direct sunlight.

Cold drafts can also be deadly. Keep your guinea pig's cage away from doors and windows, where winter drafts can leak in. Try to keep your guinea pig's cage off the floor during cold weather, too, since cold air tends to lie near the ground, creating drafts.

Avoid placing your guinea pig's cage in dark and damp areas. Basements and garages are not usually suitable areas for guinea pigs since these places in the home typically have minimal light, poor ventilation and excessive moisture. Garages are also dangerous because guinea pigs are sensitive to automobile exhaust.

Try to find a place in your home where your guinea pig will be able to watch the household activity without being unduly disturbed. You want your guinea pig to feel like part of the family, so his cage needs to be in a room where people come and go. However, don't put him in such a busy spot that he will never be able to rest or relax. Be especially careful not to place the cage near a television set, stereo or radio. A guinea pig's hearing is very sensitive, and constant noise can be very disturbing.

Guinea Pig-Proofing

Because guinea pigs are gnawing mammals and have an innate need to chew, it is vitally important that you guinea pig-proof your home before you let your pet run loose. Guinea pigs will chew on electrical cords, carpeting and anything made of wood. Along with providing your guinea pig with toys that he can chew on, you'll also need to devise ways to keep your guinea pig from gnawing on household items, for the sake of your home and the animal's health.

Make sure the space in which your guinea pig plays is free from household plants and other potentially dangerous objects.

Electrical cords pose the greatest threat to the safety of your guinea pig and should be a primary concern. Guinea pigs will chew through electrical cords, electrocuting themselves and causing a fire hazard in your home. You can protect your home and your guinea pig by moving dangling cords out of reach. Cords that cannot be moved should be covered with plastic aquarium-type tubing. To do this, slit the tubing lengthwise and put the cord inside of it. Or try wrapping the cord with spiral cable wrap, available in electronics stores.

Wooden corners and other chewable areas that will be attractive to your guinea pig can be covered with thick plastic or treated with an odoriferous substance. Perfume and cologne are repugnant to guinea pigs, who have a sharp sense of smell. You could also use store-bought repellents made to keep away other pets. Not all guinea pigs will be rebuffed by this, however, and you may have to resort to covering areas with unchewable surfaces.

Another important aspect to guinea pig-proofing your home is to take a survey of all the places where your guinea pig could get caught or hide. Since guinea pigs are inquisitive animals, your pet will want to explore every nook and cranny of your house. Look around for guinea pig-sized spaces that your pet can escape through or get trapped in. Block off these areas securely. And while you are surveying the house, make sure that toxic household chemicals and trash bags are well hidden from your pet.

Litter Box Training

Some guinea pigs can be trained to use a litter box, although they are not as good at it as rabbits. If you would like to try litter box training your guinea pig, have patience and accept the fact that your pet may never be one hundred percent reliable.

The guinea pig's denning instinct makes him a candidate for litter box training. Guinea pigs, just like cats and dogs, prefer not to foul the area where they eat and sleep, and will instead venture out of their "dens" to relieve themselves.

The most important things to remember when litter box training a guinea pig is consistency and praise. Never scold your guinea pig for not using the litter box, since this will only frighten and confuse him. Another important point is to work gradually, starting out your guinea pig in a small space and hopefully moving up to give him run of the whole house.

Most guinea pig owners use organic cat litter for their guinea pig's litter box, especially brands made from paper, wheat or grass. Stay away from clay- and wood-based litters, since these tend to be dusty and can cause respiratory problems for guinea pigs. Some pet supply stores specializing in small mammals will carry litter made just for them. This variety is the best type to buy. You can also use straw on top of a layer of newspaper as litter, although it will be less absorbent than most commercially made brands.

START SMALL

Start the litter box training process in a very small area, preferably the guinea pig's cage. Place a small litter box (the same type used for cats) in a corner of your pet's cage, attached to the side with a clip or twistable wire for removal when cleaning. Try to place the box

in the area of the cage that your guinea pig tends to use as a bathroom. Put some fecal pellets in the box to help give him the right idea, and then add a handful of hay (see Chapter 7, "Nutrition and Grooming") to a corner of the box to encourage your guinea pig to use it.

Try to keep an eye on your guinea pig while he is in his cage. When you see him defecate in the litter box, offer him a treat as a reward (see

Clever guinea pigs can be taught to use the litter box, though owners must keep in mind that this training is rarely one hundred percent effective.

Chapter 7, "Nutrition and Grooming," for suitable treats). Don't be alarmed if the guinea pig sits in the box and munches on the hay you've placed in it, since guinea pigs will often eat and defecate simultaneously. Munching on the hay will stimulate your guinea pig's digestive system and may cause him to use the box as you intended.

If your guinea pig prefers to sleep in his litter box rather than use it as a toilet, you may want to provide him with a more attractive bed than the one he has. Try using a different bedding material.

Once your guinea pig seems to be using the litter box in his cage and has been allowed to do so for some time, you can try giving him a little more space. Create a special part of the house just for him. (Kitchens, bathrooms or hallways work best.) Use a baby gate to section off a small area so you can still keep an eye on your pet.

Place the litter box in the small area, along with the guinea pig's food, water and bedding. Watch your guinea pig to make sure he uses the litter box on a regular basis. If he is using the litter box successfully, you can increase the amount of space in the house that is accessible to him.

If your guinea pig starts making mistakes at any point in the process, then it may have been too soon to place him in a bigger area. Return him to his cage and start over. Or, you may want to try buying a few more litter boxes and placing them in various parts of the guinea pig's space. With many litter box options to choose from, he is more likely to get the right idea.

> **GUINEA PIGS AND PLANTS**
>
> The following are some plants that you must take care not to let your guinea pig have access to:
>
> • Daffodil
>
> • Tulip
>
> • Lily of the Valley
>
> On the other hand, some plants are downright tasty and nutritious for your guinea pig. Consider allowing him small portions of these as a treat:
>
> • Clover
>
> • Dandelion
>
> • Mallow
>
> • Shepherd's Purse
>
> • Yarrow

CLEANING UP

While your guinea pig is learning to use the litter box, clean up after him by picking up fecal pellets with a tissue and washing urine marks on carpeting with a mixture of vinegar and water. Urine on wood floors can be cleaned simply with soap and water.

When it's time to clean your guinea pig's litter box (once or twice a week), use a water and vinegar solution and dry it thoroughly before filling it with litter and returning it to its usual spot.

Remember that your guinea pig may never learn to use the litter box reliably and will more than likely have occasional accidents. Patience, understanding and a sense of humor will help you cope with this situation. Try to come up with ideas on how to adapt to your guinea pig's bathroom habits.

chapter 6

Outdoor
Guinea Pigs

If keeping your guinea pig indoors is out of the question, it is possible to successfully house her outside if you take strict precautions. Before you prepare to bring your outdoor guinea pig home with you, be sure to check your local zoning ordinances to make certain it is legal to keep a guinea pig outdoors in your area. Failing to do so could result in trouble with your neighbors and eventual difficulties with authorities.

When determining what kind of housing you will provide for your guinea pig and where it will be located, there are many details you must keep in mind so your guinea pig is healthy and safe.

65

You will need to protect your guinea pig from the elements, as well as from extreme changes in temperature. You will also need to guard against predators, and allow your guinea pig enough room to move around comfortably.

The Hutch

There are a number of commercially made hutches available that are suitable for guinea pigs. It's important to choose a hutch that will meet your guinea pig's needs for shelter, comfort and safety.

SIZE

First, consider size. The more room you can provide for your guinea pig, the better. Buy your guinea pig the largest hutch your allotted space will accommodate. Giving your guinea pig plenty of room to move around will help her stay happy and healthy.

When determining suitable living space for a guinea pig, keep your pet's size in mind. A good rule of thumb when determining the minimum living room your guinea pig will need is to calculate 100 square inches of floor space for each adult guinea pig. However, it's preferable to give your guinea pig even more room than that. A guinea pig who does not have enough room in her hutch may become depressed. A space that's too small will be fouled more quickly with feces and urine, leaving the guinea pig to spend more time than she should in unsanitary conditions, and making cleanup a bigger hassle for you. On the other hand, don't get a single-door hutch that is so deep you can't reach into it to clean it. Large hutches should have more than one door.

You'll also want to make sure that the hutch is big enough to accommodate a separate sleeping space, either in the form of a nest box or a built-in

> **A COOLING TIP**
>
> To protect your guinea pig from overheating in the summertime, put plastic jugs of frozen water in the hutch that your guinea pig can lie against to keep cool. Keep a few of these jugs in your freezer so you can rotate them once the ice melts.

compartment. Providing your guinea pig with a secluded and separate place to sleep will help her feel safer and happier in the hutch. A built-in sleeping compartment should be about 1½ feet long and half a foot in height and width.

Larger hutches can also accommodate litter boxes. (See Chapter 5, "Indoor Guinea Pigs" for information on litter box training.) If you'd like your guinea pig to spend free-roaming time with you inside your home, you may want to try to litter box train her, and then have her use a litter box even in her hutch. This way, she will be used to using the box and will be less likely to have an accident when she has free run of the house.

MATERIALS

Most hutches are made from either wood and wire or just wire. Each has its advantages and disadvantages.

Wooden hutches usually consist of a wooden roof and wood-panel sides, with wire mesh on the door, front and/or some sides of the cage. Wooden hutches stay cooler in the summer and warmer in the winter, providing they are made with a good quality wood and not pressboard. They can also be very attractive.

One problem with wooden hutches is that the wood can eventually rot, causing the hutch to slowly fall apart. Another disadvantage to wood is that guinea pigs love to chew on it, and can gnaw sections of a wooden hutch to pieces if the wood is not protected by wire mesh.

Metal hutches, on the other hand, have the disadvantage of retaining heat in the summer and cold in the winter, which can be harmful to the guinea pig inside. Metal hutches are very durable, however, and can last a very long time if they are well-made. They are also easier to clean than wood hutches, and often are less expensive.

Whether you choose a wooden hutch or a wire hutch, it's important to select a home for your guinea pig that utilizes the proper type of wire. Chicken wire is not acceptable, since it is flimsy and easily removed by both predators and the guinea pigs themselves. Side panels and doors on both wooden and metal hutches should be made from sturdy, galvanized wire, around 14-gauge in weight. The size of the holes in the wire mesh should be no larger than 1 inch by 2 inches.

The roof of an outdoor hutch should be covered with a waterproof substance, such as heavy-duty plastic or roofing material. This is vital if the hutch and its occupant are to stay warm and dry in inclement weather.

Floor material is very important. Improper flooring can cause a number of health problems in your guinea pig. Most hutches have some wire flooring, designed to allow feces and urine to drop away from the animal. However, wire mesh that is too large can be dangerous since a guinea pig's leg can fall through. The wire mesh should also be smooth because a rough edge can result in sore hocks.

This hutch has a piece of wood as part of the flooring, which allows the guinea pig to have a break from the wire.

Make sure at least one-third of the floor space contains a flat, porous surface (preferably wood) where your guinea pig can sit to get off the wire. This is important, since constant walking on wire can cause sore hocks.

DESIGN

When considering which hutch to purchase for an outdoor guinea pig, the factors of guinea pig health, safety and comfort mentioned above obviously come into play. Beyond this, however, the choice of design in a hutch is a matter of individual preference based on convenience, quality and aesthetic appeal.

The first feature to look at in hutch design is quality. Does the hutch appear to be well built? Is it made from quality materials? Look to see that the welding was done before the metal was galvanized. Check the hinges and various connections throughout the hutch to determine whether or not they are well put together. Examine the construction carefully to make sure that the hutch is secure and escape-proof. Feel around the hutch for sharp points. Unfinished edges indicate sloppy craftsmanship and a potential danger to your guinea pig.

Another element to consider is height. Some hutches are made low to the ground, while others have legs that put them anywhere from several inches to several feet off the ground. Cages should not rest directly on the ground. For better ventilation and sanitation, hutches should be at least six inches off the ground. Hutches that rest directly on soil may end up being homes for mice and rats, who will create nests underneath the floor. If you purchase a hutch with no legs, you'll have to create some means of raising it up so air can pass underneath. It's best if the bottom of the cage is waist-high. This makes the hutch easier to clean, and makes access to the guinea pig less difficult for you.

This hutch is well crafted and properly placed out of direct sunlight.

When it comes to convenience, the location and style of doors are also important factors in hutch design. Outdoor hutches usually have doors on the front of the cage, although some will have top-opening entries. Unless your hutch is very low to the ground, you will want to purchase a design that has a door in the front. This will make it easier to reach in for cleaning.

To ensure that the hutch fits the needs of their pets, many guinea pig owners will design and build their own outdoor hutches. If you choose to do this, you may want to contact your local county extension office or the American Rabbit Breeders Association for plans and further information on how to construct a safe and sturdy hutch.

LOCATION

Temperature and Sunlight   Heat is more dangerous to guinea pigs than cold, so when choosing a location for your cage, make sure it is in a shady spot. This is particularly important if you live in a warm climate. Guinea pigs evolved to live underground in burrows. Exposing them to direct sun or extreme heat can easily kill them. Temperatures above 85 degrees are considered dangerous for guinea pigs, especially if accompanied by high humidity.

On the other hand, you don't want to keep your guinea pig in total darkness. In fact, guinea pigs need long periods of light in order to sleep, since they are nocturnal. The location you pick must get sufficient sunlight that does not shine directly on the hutch.

While guinea pigs are more able to tolerate the cold, they should be protected from drafts. Guinea pigs who are subjected to constant wind or drafts will eventually become sick, since their immune systems will be compromised by the stress on their bodies. Choose a protected location for your guinea pig hutch, out of drafts and wind. Placing a hutch alongside a building can often provide defense from the wind.

Dampness is a killer when it comes to guinea pigs. Even though your guinea pig will be outside, you will have to make sure that she stays dry. Hot, humid weather can cause moldy, unsanitary conditions in the nesting box, and rain or snow can drench a guinea pig and her entire bed. Even though your hutch will have a waterproof roof, you must place it in a location where it will be sheltered from rain, snow and excessive dampness.

Temperatures that rise and fall rapidly in short periods of time are not good for guinea pigs either. If you live in a climate where the days are hot and the nights are cold, your outdoor guinea pig will suffer. Since there is little you can do to protect an outdoor guinea pig from these kinds of temperature extremes, it is best to keep your pet's cage indoors during the harshest times of the year.

Ventilation   This is also an important factor in hutch placement. Caged guinea pigs need plenty of fresh air since a stuffy environment can wreak havoc on a guinea pig's respiratory system. The ammonia from the guinea pig's urine and the dust from her bedding can cause respiratory distress and infection, causing the animal to become sick and even die. Make sure you select a spot that is well ventilated while still protected from the elements.

Noise Pollution   Don't place your hutch in a place where there is excessive noise. Guinea pigs need to sleep during the day and will become nervous and stressed if there are frequent loud noises or disturbances.

Convenience and Security   When choosing a spot for your guinea pig's home, keep in mind that you will need to have convenient access to it so you can clean it regularly, give food to your guinea pig and take your guinea pig out daily for exercise and companionship.

When determining the location for your outdoor hutch, it is vital to always remember that guinea pigs are prey animals, and will attract any number of predators. Dogs and cats are only two of the creatures that will be drawn to your yard once a guinea pig is in place. Depending on where you live, raccoons, coyotes, hawks, owls and even weasels may try to get to your guinea pig.

Providing a secure hutch does not necessarily mean that your guinea pig will be safe. Raccoons are known to prey on small mammals, and can reach through the wire of a hutch and kill a guinea pig. Other animals can kill your guinea pig by frightening her to death even though they can't actually get at it. Guinea pigs can go into fatal shock from fear alone.

It's difficult to provide an outdoor guinea pig with both physical and psychological protection from predators without actually building an enclosed fence around her hutch. However, if you want to ensure that your guinea pig is safe from other animals, you will need to do this. The purpose behind the enclosure is not only to keep predators from gaining access to your guinea pig's cage, but also to keep them far enough away so that they don't frighten your guinea pig.

Guinea pig cages can be kept on apartment terraces as long as the space is protected in the same ways as a backyard. Provide shade for the hutch and safeguards from climbing predators, as well as protection from drafts and temperature extremes.

This outdoor enclosure makes a perfect guinea pig playground.

Outdoor Guinea Pig Care

Guinea pigs who are housed outdoors need special attention. Because your guinea pig is not living inside the home with you, you will need to make an extra effort to observe her and spend time with her. You will also have to make sure her outdoor environment is well tended.

OBSERVATION

One of the most important aspects of outdoor guinea pig care is observation. Because signs of illness can often be subtle at the onset of a disease, it is vital that you keep a close watch on your guinea pig. Early treatment of an illness can often mean the difference between life or death for an animal. Learn to know how she behaves when she is feeling good so you can immediately recognize when there is a problem. Check on her frequently throughout the day to see how she is doing.

You'll need to make an extra effort to observe your outdoor guinea pig for signs of disease and illness.

EXERCISE

It's important that your guinea pig receive daily exercise. If you cannot bring her inside the house to play, then you'll have to provide her with a completely enclosed run in the backyard to stretch her legs (the bigger the better, with four feet being the minimum length). Or, use an empty plastic wading pool and let your pet run around in it and play with her toys.

If your yard is enclosed by walls or a sturdy fence with no holes that a guinea pig can slip through, you may give your pet the run of the yard. However, a guinea pig should never run loose without supervision since she may fall victim to a predator (including birds like owls or hawks that can swoop down from the sky) or poisonous plants in your yard.

SOCIAL INTERACTION

Since guinea pigs are such highly social creatures, an outdoor guinea pig living alone in a hutch can suffer terribly from loneliness. For this reason, you will need to make a concerted effort to provide her with social interaction. Bring her in the house as often as you can so she can spend time with you. Sit in the backyard with her as she plays in her run or in the yard. And if you don't have a lot of time to do this, get another guinea pig to keep her company in her hutch.

If you let your guinea pig loose in the yard, make sure she avoids potential dangers like poisonous plants.

REGULAR CLEANING

Outdoor hutches get dirty quickly, and for your guinea pig's health and well-being, you'll need to clean your hutch frequently. While you can get away with not cleaning it every day, it wouldn't hurt to do so.

Before you clean the hutch, remove your guinea pig and put her in a safe place. (A travel carrier is useful for this purpose.) Don't let her roam about unsupervised; she may get into trouble while you are working.

Because guinea pigs normally live in dens, they tend to use the same area of their hutch as a toilet. Using a spatula and hand shovel, scrape away the feces and urine that build up in that area. Once a week, you should also scrub the area until it is clean using a hard-bristle brush and water containing a splash of bleach. Wait until the inside of the hutch is completely dry before placing the guinea pig back in.

While you are cleaning the hutch, use the opportunity to inspect the inside for damage or ill repair.

chapter 7

Nutrition
and
Grooming

Guinea pigs are relatively easy pets to care for once you have taken the time to learn about their health requirements. Guinea pigs are rodents, and have different dietary needs from humans and other pets.

Feeding Your Guinea Pig

The way you feed your guinea pig can mean the difference between a healthy, long-lived pet and a sickly, unhappy animal. Guinea pigs are herbivores, and their nutritional requirements are unique.

In nature, the guinea pig is a browser, an animal who spends considerable amounts of time foraging for and eating plants. Because plant material is difficult to break down, the digestive tract of the guinea pig is uniquely constructed.

It's important to give your guinea pig a diet that simulates the diet he would eat in the wild. Failure to do so will result in a guinea pig with chronic diarrhea; heart, liver and kidney disease; and obesity.

PELLETS

People usually think of pelleted feed as something that only rabbits eat, but specially made pellets just for guinea pigs are available. When supplemented with fresh foods, these pellets provide balanced nutrition for the guinea pig. Guinea pigs, unlike most other mammals, are unable to manufacture vitamin C within their bodies and need a higher amount of folic acid, so it's important to feed them only pellets made especially for guinea pigs because these pellets contain those nutrients.

When you purchase a pelleted guinea pig feed at your pet supply store, look for a product that contains at least 8 percent protein, 16 percent fiber, and 1 gram of vitamin C per kilogram. Read the packaging to be sure the pellets are labeled as nutritionally complete.

Do not buy a large supply of pellets, since they will lose their nutritional value with time. Purchase as much as your guinea pig will consume in about a month. Store the food in the refrigerator where they will stay fresher longer.

If your guinea pig is young (less than three months old), you may leave a bowl of pellets in his cage at all times for him to eat when he wishes. However, if you have an adult, you should provide two servings of 2 tablespoons each day. Feeding the animal once in the morning and once in the evening is ideal. If the guinea pig starts to become obese, you may have to cut back to 1 tablespoon per day. You may also want to try increasing his exercise time.

If your guinea pig does not eat the pellets you place in his dish, throw the old ones away before you refill the bowl. It's important to offer only fresh pellets.

HAY

When you purchased your guinea pig's cage or hutch, you also bought a hay rack. Guinea pigs need free access to fibrous foods, and hay, which is pure roughage, fits the bill.

Hay can be obtained from a number of sources, including pet supply stores, feed stores and local horse stables. When you purchase hay, check it for freshness. Good, clean hay should have a sweet smell and minimal dust. Examine it for mold, which can be very harmful to guinea pigs if ingested. Do not purchase hay that is wet or damp. When you get it home, store the hay in a cool place protected from rain or dampness.

There are different types of hay available. Your pet supply store will stock packaged alfalfa and timothy hay, while feed stores and stables will have baled hay. Timothy hay is generally the best. If your guinea pig is eating pellets, alfalfa hay is already included in his diet. The addition of more alfalfa may cause him to become overweight. (Hay cubes, manufactured for horses, are not recommended for guinea pigs.)

Give your guinea pig a handful of fresh hay every day to keep his digestive system in working order. Place the hay in the hay rack to help keep it from scattering around the cage. Remove old hay from the cage and the rack before you replace it with new hay.

FEEDING TIPS

• Wash your guinea pig's food dish every so often to prevent bacteria buildup.

• Feed your animal pellets formulated especially for guinea pigs as a dietary staple.

• Offer a variety of fresh greens daily.

• Stick to a regular feeding schedule for your guinea pig. Once in the morning and once in the evening is ideal.

• Make sure your guinea pig has access to fresh hay.

• Keep a water bottle filled with fresh water at all times. Check it frequently, especially in the summer, to make sure there is an ample supply.

GREENS

Pellets and hay are not the only foodstuffs that you'll need to give your guinea pig. Fresh greens are also an important dietary element that should be provided daily.

Some of the best fresh foods for guinea pigs include dark green plants such as romaine lettuce, dandelions, carrot tops, broccoli, basil, spinach and artichokes. Many other leafy green vegetables that humans eat are good for guinea pigs, too, provided the leaves are dark green in color. Dark green leaves provide the guinea pig with valuable vitamin C, which the animal cannot manufacture on his own.

Romaine lettuce is one of the best fresh foods to offer your guinea pig.

Make sure the greens you offer your guinea pig are fresh. Purchase them from the produce department of your supermarket or from a farm stand, and be sure to wash them thoroughly to remove residual pesticides. Do not gather the greens from fields unless you can be completely certain that they have not been sprayed with chemicals and that they are not poisonous. Organically grown greens, if you can find them, are by far the best choice for guinea pigs.

Growing Them Yourself

You may want to consider growing a garden for your guinea pig, where he can forage for greens as nature intended. Good garden plants that are healthy for guinea pigs include coltsfoot, dandelion, dead-nettles, ground elder, mugwort, plantain, ragwort, shepherd's purse and yarrow. Guinea pigs also like to nibble on Bermuda grass and clover.

To create a guinea pig garden, set aside a patch of your backyard and plant the seeds of some of the plants

79

mentioned earlier. Be sure to use organic soil and no pesticides. When the plants are mature, create a protective enclosure for your guinea pig. Then let your guinea pig run loose among the plants to graze to his heart's content. As you supervise him, you'll have the opportunity to see your guinea pig's wild side as he expresses his natural browsing instincts. (A note of caution: There are many common plants that are poisonous, so your pet's foraging should be restricted to plants that are known to be safe.)

If your guinea pig is a strictly indoor pet, you can grow some of these same plants in a large tray on your balcony or fire escape, bring the tray inside every so often, and let your guinea pig munch on them. He will enjoy the opportunity to harvest his own greens, and you will have fun observing him.

Let your guinea pig visit the garden or tray once or twice a week. On the other days, be sure to provide him with different greens than the ones you are growing so he will have diversity in his diet.

If your guinea pig is not used to eating fresh foods, you should introduce them gradually to his diet so the animal does not get diarrhea. Start by offering him one new item of food once a week. Eventually, your guinea pig should be receiving three different types of fresh greens daily, making up no more than 15 percent of his diet. Remember to promptly remove uneaten greens from your guinea pig's cage.

Grow clover in your garden or in a window box and offer the fresh leaves to your guinea pig.

You may find that your guinea pig has a sensitivity to a particular vegetable. You'll know because he will get diarrhea not long after he eats it. Should this happen, remove the offending food from his diet.

TREATS

Guinea pigs enjoy receiving occasional treats. Feeding treats to your guinea pig will help the two of you bond, and will supplement his diet.

The healthiest treats to feed your guinea pig are fresh fruits. Some of the treats guinea pigs enjoy include oranges, apples, pears, strawberries, peaches and tomatoes. While these items are particularly popular among guinea pigs, you can offer your pet just about any fruit. Just be sure to feed in moderation. (Carrots, though not a fruit, are also a guinea pig favorite.)

Commercially prepared treats can also be acceptable for guinea pigs, as long as the treats are not overfed. Avoid giving your guinea pig commercial treats that contain sugar. It's also wise to refrain from offering your pet traditional human treats that are high in sugar or salt, including candy and chocolate.

Occasionally, you may also want to give your guinea pig some dried and aged twigs from an unsprayed fruit tree as a treat. Guinea pigs love to gnaw on branches and sometimes rip off the bark and eat it. (Drying and aging is important since some tree branches are poisonous when fresh.)

CECOTROPES

Several decades ago, researchers discovered that some small mammals have an unusual way of supplementing their diets. Small, soft pellets known as cecotropes are produced by the guinea pig's cecum (a part of the large intestine). These cecotropes, which contain special nutrients, pass from the anus and are then instinctively eaten by the guinea pig. While this may seem very strange to us, nature developed this system to help the guinea pig absorb nutrients from the hard-to-digest cellulose material contained in plants.

In order for your guinea pig to get the most nutrition from his diet, he must be able to consume an adequate amount of the cecotropes produced by his body. Since these pellets are usually ingested just as they leave the anus, you may occasionally see your guinea pig eating them as they are produced. Do not discourage him.

SALT LICK

While many pet supply stores stock salt licks for use in small mammal cages, most guinea pigs do not need a salt block if they are on a diet that includes pellets. Nutritionally complete pellets made for guinea pigs include enough salt. Providing a salt block cannot hurt your guinea pig, however, and you can offer him one to see if he likes it.

WATER

Water is very important to the guinea pig, as it is to any living creature, and should be provided at all times. Change your guinea pig's water daily and wash the water bottle out on a regular basis. Be sure to keep a close eye on the water level in your guinea pig's bottle in the summer or whenever he is exposed to heat.

VITAMIN SUPPLEMENTS

In addition to providing green leafy produce for your guinea pig, you can also supplement his vitamin C intake by adding 100 milligrams of ascorbic acid in the form of a syrup or tablet (the kind made for humans works well) in each cup of drinking water that you give your guinea pig.

Grooming

One of the first things you will notice when you start living with your guinea pig is that he loves to groom himself. Guinea pigs are much like cats in that respect, always preening and primping.

Even though your guinea pig loves to groom himself, he will also appreciate regular grooming from you. Grooming can help in the bonding process, and will also provide you with a chance to look your guinea pig over for any signs of parasites or ill health.

It is best to set aside an hour one day a week for grooming your guinea pig. (Longhaired breeds must be groomed daily.) Gather your grooming tools and find a comfortable spot where you can sit with your guinea pig on your lap. While you are preparing to brush the animal, it is a good time to check eyes and ears for discharge and examine the bottoms of his feet for sores.

Guinea pigs tend to shed more at certain times of the year. In the early fall, hair begins to fall out in larger quantities than normal. In the winter, the shed hairs are replaced by more fur that will help keep the animal warm. During the shedding seasons, it is best to brush your pet at least every other day.

Guinea pigs, like cats, enjoy grooming themselves regularly.

BRUSHING

Begin your grooming session by brushing or combing your guinea pig. You will notice a lot of loose hairs are coming out. Since guinea pigs tend to shed at any time of year, this is normal.

When you are brushing and combing your pet, keep an eye out for parasites such as lice and mites. Lice are small, flattened insects, and their presence is usually accompanied by itching, scratching and hair loss.

Mites are microscopic, but also cause itching, hair loss and scabby skin. If you suspect that there may be lice or mites on your pet, contact your veterinarian. He or she can provide you with safe chemicals designed to kill lice and mites, and give you details on how to eliminate these parasites from your guinea pig's environment.

As you brush or comb your guinea pig, keep an eye out for any lumps or sores on the animal's body that could be an indication of disease or infection.

If your guinea pig has long hair, you will need to use your brush to work out any mats you may find in his coat. Regular, careful grooming will prevent mats from forming. Another option for longhaired guinea pigs is to have them trimmed by a professional groomer experienced in handling guinea pigs.

When you are brushing your guinea pig, keep an eye out for lice and mites.

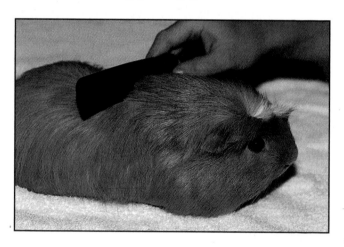

TRIMMING TOENAILS

Trimming your guinea pig's toenails is also a necessary part of your grooming sessions, although it will not need to be done every week. Check the length and condition of your guinea pig's nails every time you groom him. Once the nails appear to be getting long, it is time to trim them.

Prepare to trim your guinea pig's nails by placing him gently in your lap with his legs facing upward. Use your clipper to take off a portion of the nail. Be careful not to cut the quick in the toenail; doing so can cause pain to the guinea pig and a bloody toenail. A silhouette of the quick can seen by holding the nail up to a light.

If you are nervous about trimming your guinea pig's nails for the first time, or if your guinea pig struggles when you try to hold him in your lap, you may want to ask your veterinarian to show you how to perform this necessary function.

Although you might be tempted at times, try to avoid giving your guinea pig a bath. As a rule, guinea pigs don't enjoy being bathed and rarely need to be bathed unless they are show animals. If your guinea pig needs his bottom cleaned, try to cleanse it with soap and water without submerging the entire guinea pig in water. Once you have finished, make sure the guinea pig is completely dry before you put him back in his cage since a wet bottom and feet can attract egg-laying flies on outdoor guinea pigs or result in sores on the skin.

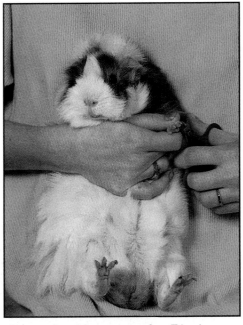

Trimming your guinea pig's toenails is a necessary part of his grooming regimen.

chapter 8

Keeping Your
Guinea Pig
Healthy

Guinea pigs who are well fed and properly cared for rarely get sick. However, if a guinea pig's basic needs, including a proper diet, a clean environment and regular exercise, are not met, the animal becomes susceptible to a number of dangerous illnesses. In other words, taking good care of your guinea pig will pay off in a healthy pet. And, since many guinea pig ailments are difficult to cure, prevention is the best policy.

Guinea Pig Anatomy

The body of the guinea pig is the result of her wild ancestors' evolution and adaptations. The anatomy of the guinea pig is designed to allow the animal to carry out her most important functions: eating, reproducing and fleeing from predators.

The guinea pig has a short, stocky body, no tail and large eyes. The front feet are flat, and usually have four digits with claws. The hind feet have three digits with claws, and are much longer than the front feet. Full-grown, domestic guinea pigs weigh between 2 and 3 pounds, and measure about 10 inches in length.

THE COAT

The domestic guinea pig comes in a variety of colors, thanks to the handiwork of man. Natural selection played no part in the varied patterns of the domestic guinea pig, with the exception of one: the agouti coloration. Agouti is the color nature gave the guinea pig to help conceal it in the wild.

Regardless of color, all guinea pigs' coats are made up of large, coarse guard hairs and an undercoat of finer hair. Each hair on the guinea pig's body has a follicle, which is located near a sebaceous gland. The guinea pig's sebaceous glands provide oil to the skin and coat to keep it healthy.

The guinea pig's entire body is covered with hair except for her ear flaps and the pads of her feet. Five or six rows of whiskers are located on each side of the guinea pig's nose.

BONES AND MUSCLES

The guinea pig's skeleton and muscular structure give the animal her plant-eating abilities and speed for quick getaways. The thirty-four vertebrae and thirteen to fourteen ribs provide the primary frame of the guinea pig's body. This frame supports a relatively large skull, which makes up about one-third of the guinea pig's total body weight.

The guinea pig's dentition is very important to its survival. With twenty teeth in all, the guinea pig has chisel-like incisors and rootless molars. All these teeth continue to grow throughout the animal's life to compensate for the fact that they wear down through constant use.

The muscles that cover the skeleton of the guineapig are called skeletal muscles. These muscles are what enable the guinea pig to move rapidly and do all the other physical activities typical of guinea pigs.

The most impressive muscles on the guinea pig's body are the masticatory muscles, located on the jaw. These muscles enable the guinea pig to gnaw on husks, pods and shells to get to the seeds inside, and to grind this tough food down into fine particles. These are necessary requirements for an animal whose entire diet consists of plant material.

GUINEA PIG TEETH

Like all rodents, your guinea pig's teeth are constantly growing. She needs to chew on something hard, like a block of untreated wood, to keep them properly worn down. In a condition called malocclusion, a guinea pig's teeth are misaligned and she can't wear them down properly. If you notice that your guinea pig's teeth don't fit together (the top teeth should overlap the lower) take her to the vet, who will properly recommend regular trimming of the teeth or their removal.

DIGESTIVE SYSTEM

The guinea pig's gastrointestinal system is designed to efficiently digest plant fiber, and is able to turn 80 percent of the food she eats into energy. The process begins with the softening of the food in the animal's stomach, from which it moves down into the large intestine. From here it goes to a part of the guinea pig's anatomy called the cecum. Similar to a human appendix, the cecum is on the left side of the guinea pig's body and makes up about 15 percent of the animal's entire weight. The cecum's function is to house bacteria that can break down the cellulose in the plant matter eaten by the guinea pig. The cellulose is turned into carbohydrate constituents, which are digestible.

Before the guinea pig can obtain the nutrients from the matter digested in the cecum, the food material must return to the stomach. This is achieved through a process called refection. The guinea pig expels the material in pellet form from the anus, and then eats it. Once the pellet gets to the stomach, the carbohydrates are absorbed.

REPRODUCTION

Guinea pigs are known for their ability to reproduce quickly and prolifically. This is one of the reasons for their popularity as a food animal in South American cultures.

The female guinea pig becomes able to breed at the age of seven weeks, although the healthiest young are produced when she has reached twelve weeks of age. Males are ready to breed when they are only two weeks old.

Females go into heat every thirteen to twenty-one days. Babies are born anywhere from fifty-six to seventy-four days after breeding. Litters usually range from one to thirteen babies, but four is most typical. The female guinea pig has only two teats with which to nurse her young, so many of the babies born to very large litters often do not survive.

The young are born with furry bodies and with their eyes open, and are able to eat solid food within a day after being born. They are weaned within three weeks to a month after birth, making them self-sufficient creatures at an early age.

Disease Prevention

If you follow the feeding and housing guidelines outlined in this book, your guinea pig should live a long and healthy life. However, you can ensure this even more by taking extra precautions to ward off illness and deal with problems effectively, should they come up.

DIET

Probably the single most important step you can take to make sure that your guinea pig stays healthy is to feed her a proper diet. In order for the body systems to work properly, your guinea pig needs to eat certain foods (see Chapter 7, "Nutrition and Grooming," for complete information on nutritional requirements). A correctly functioning system will help your guinea pig ward off a number of afflictions that often trouble less well-kept animals.

When changing your guinea pig's diet or adding a new food, remember to always do so gradually. A sudden alteration of what your pet is eating can wreak havoc on her digestive system and cause her to become seriously ill.

An extremely important element in your guinea pig's diet is water. Your guinea pig should always have access to clean, fresh water to keep her body functioning properly. Lack of water can result in a number of life-threatening conditions in guinea pigs.

Keeping your guinea pig's environment clean is an easy way to help prevent diseases.

CLEANLINESS

Another vitally important factor in keeping your guinea pig healthy is cleanliness. An unsanitary cage is a breeding ground for disease. A number of different illnesses can be directly traced to dirty floors and nest boxes and unclean food bowls and water bottles. Remove fouled bedding and fecal matter daily, and wash your cage or hutch once a week to keep bacteria at a minimum. Scrub your guinea pig's food dish and water bottle every day.

STRESS

Like humans, guinea pigs are susceptible to stress. But unlike most humans, your guinea pig cannot do much to change her life and alleviate the stress. She relies on you to do it for her.

Stress has serious consequences on the body's immune system. You may have noticed that when you are under a lot of stress, you tend to catch colds more easily. The same is true for guinea pigs, although the ailments they catch can be much more dangerous than the common cold.

So keep your guinea pig's stress to a minimum. This means that the animal should not be exposed to loud noises, excessive handling, severe temperature changes and situations that will frighten her. Guinea pigs also need regular exercise and companionship, and providing these will reduce the amount of stress in your pet's life. Keeping stress to a minimum will result in a guinea pig with a healthy immune system that is able to fight off the various bacteria, fungus and parasites to which she may be exposed.

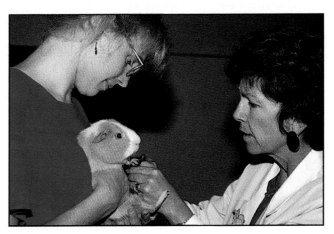

Once you have found a veterinarian who treats guinea pigs, take your pet in for a checkup.

FIND A VETERINARIAN

Many people think only cats and dogs need to go to a veterinarian. This is not true. Small mammals, such as guinea pigs, should receive veterinary treatment whenever they become ill or injured.

Since your guinea pig's body differs considerably from that of a cat or dog, some of the treatments and medications appropriate for these other pets could be harmful to your guinea pig. In fact, certain antibiotics commonly given to other small animals can kill a guinea pig. Given this, it's important to only use a vet who has experience in treating guinea pigs.

No matter what kind of pet you own, it's best not to wait until you have an emergency on your hands to go looking for a veterinarian. Since vets who specialize in treating guinea pigs are harder to find than traditional animal doctors, it is wise to select your guinea pig's veterinarian before she actually needs one.

The best way to find a guinea pig vet is by referral. Ask other guinea pig owners who they use, and whether or not they are happy with that individual or clinic. Speak to the breeder or rescuer who provided you with your

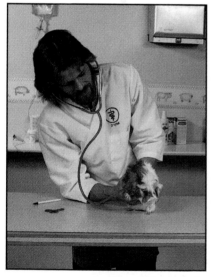

guinea pig. If you don't know any other guinea pig owners near you, contact the House Rabbit Society (listed in Chapter 12, "Resources"). They can help you locate a guinea pig vet in your area. Or call your local county extension office and get the name and number of the guinea pig 4-H project leader in your area. He or she should be able to refer you to a veterinarian who treats guinea pigs.

Once you have selected a veterinarian, you may want to take your new guinea pig in for an exami-

If you notice any unusual behavior in your guinea pig, don't hesitate to visit the veterinarian.

nation. The veterinarian will be able to tell you if your pet has any potential health problems, and set up an appointment for a spay or neuter, if you desire to have this surgery performed. This meeting will also give you an opportunity to get to know the vet and give him or her the chance to start a file on your pet. This may also be a good time to ask your vet to show you how to clip your guinea pig's nails and answer any questions you may have on how to care for your new pet.

Get to know your guinea pig, and keep a close eye on her. If you know how she looks when she is healthy, you'll be more likely to recognize signs of illness early on. Many diseases that can be fatal are often curable in their earliest stages. Realizing your guinea pig is under the weather before she becomes seriously ill could mean the difference between life and death.

Regular grooming is an important part of observation, since this hands-on procedure will encourage you to take a close look at your pet. The tasks required of regular grooming, such as maintenance of your pet's nails and brushing, will help you prevent serious illness and injury.

Examine your guinea pig's cage floor or litter box regularly. Keep an eye out for diarrhea or lack of feces, both of which can indicate a possible problem.

Common Ailments

There are quite a few illnesses that affect a guinea pig, but many are rarely seen. Below is a list of the most common health problems in pet guinea pigs today.

Obesity is a common health problem in guinea pigs.

Obesity   Veterinarians indicate that obesity is a major health problem in guinea pigs. Guinea pigs who are overweight are prone to a number of illnesses affecting their major organs. The primary cause of obesity in guinea pigs is the overfeeding of pellets. Guinea pigs who are obese should be placed on a special diet to help them get down to their proper weight. If you are feeding your guinea pig too many pellets, cut back to the amount recommended in Chapter 7, "Nutrition and Grooming." If this does not result in a noticeable change in a month or so, consult your veterinarian for help.

Constipation/Diarrhea Difficulty in defecating (constipation) or very loose stools (diarrhea) can be the result of poor diet or another illness. Symptoms of constipation are straining to defecate, lack of feces, distended abdomen and lethargy. Diarrhea is usually detected by loose or runny stools and a dirty bottom. Your veterinarian will need to make a determination as to what is causing the problem in either one of these cases.

Heat Prostration Guinea pigs are very susceptible to overheating. When the weather is hot, keep a close eye on your pet. Signs of heat prostration include a stretched out posture, panting, rapid breathing and slobbering. If you find your guinea pig in this state, move her to a cool place out of the sun and put a cold, wet towel around her body, or bathe her in cool water. Heat prostration is an emergency situation. Contact your veterinarian immediately.

Lice Lice are a common problem for guinea pigs. These tiny, wingless insects live in the hair of infested guinea pigs. Many pet guinea pigs suffer from light infestations of lice that are not obvious to their owners. If the infestation becomes heavy, however, the guinea pig will begin to scratch and lose hair, and scabs may form on the skin. If you suspect

---

SIGNS OF POOR HEALTH

How will you know if your guinea pig isn't feeling well? In addition to drastic changes in behavior, there are a number of telltale signs to watch for:

- A dull look in the eyes
- Lethargy
- Loss of appetite
- Constipation or diarrhea
- Discharge from the eyes or nose
- Bloated abdomen
- Labored breathing
- Unexplained weight loss

If your guinea pig exhibits any of these signs, contact your veterinarian immediately.

that your guinea pig has lice, take her to a veterinarian for diagnosis. Since guinea pig lice easily spread to other guinea pigs (but not to people), it is best to keep your healthy pet from associating with other members of her species who may be contaminated.

Mites Guinea pigs are susceptible to a specific mite called *Trixacarus cavie*. This mite causes the guinea pig to lose patches of hair, where the skin will become red and scabby. Severely infested guinea pigs will run around wildly and in circles. Trixacarus mites are easily spread from one animal to another. Contact your veterinarian for help in treating this parasite.

A healthy guinea pig is an active, playful pet.

Flies Flies can be dangerous to outdoor guinea pigs. They often lay their eggs on a guinea pig's soiled rectal area, leaving maggots to burrow in and feed on the animal's flesh. Flies can be kept at bay by ensuring that both your guinea pig's cage and her fur are kept clean. If flies do lay eggs on your guinea pig, contact a veterinarian for assistance.

Abscesses Abscesses are bacterial infections that result from a puncture wound of some kind. If your guinea pig has cut herself on something or has had a fight with another pet, she may develop an abscess at the site of the injury. You will recognize an abscess by its round appearance, usually accompanied by a discharge. Your veterinarian will need to treat your guinea pig with antibiotics to help her fight off the infection.

Worms Roundworms and tapeworms, two parasites that commonly afflict dogs and cats, also prey on guinea pigs. Symptoms of worm infestation include a distended abdomen, poor coat condition, and worms in the feces or near the anus. If you suspect that your guinea pig has worms, contact your veterinarian.

Malocclusion When a guinea pig's front teeth do not wear down properly, the condition is known as malocclusion. This problem is usually genetic, the result of teeth that are misaligned. Signs of malocclusion include overly long teeth, infections in the mouth, ulcerations on the lips or tongue and difficulty eating. This is a common problem in guinea pigs and must be handled by a veterinarian or the guinea pig will eventually die. Treatment consists of a regular trimming of the teeth, or their complete removal.

Your guinea pig's nose should be clean and free of discharge.

Sore Hocks Guinea pigs who live in a cage or hutch with a wire floor often develop sore hocks. This con-dition is typified by red, swollen skin on the hind legs with accompanying hair loss. The guinea pig may also be reluctant to move. A veterinarian will provide an antibiotic ointment for treatment, along with a recommendation for a change in flooring.

Respiratory Infections Guinea pigs are prone to a number of viruses and bacteria that can cause respiratory infections. Symptoms include sneezing, discharge from the nose and eyes, loss of appetite, lethargy and difficulty breathing. Prompt attention by a veterinarian is essential when a respiratory ailment is suspected.

Scurvy Because guinea pigs cannot manufacture their own vitamin C as many other mammals can, they are prone to scurvy, a disease caused by a deficiency in vitamin C. A guinea pig suffering from scurvy will have a poor appetite; swollen, painful joints and chest; a reluctance to move and/or bleeding from the gums. If scurvy is untreated, it can be fatal. A guinea pig with these symptoms should be taken to a veterinarian immediately.

Enjoying
Your

part three

Guinea Pig

chapter 9

Understanding
Your
Guinea Pig

In order to have a rewarding relationship with your guinea pig, it's important that you understand him. The domestic guinea pig is very similar to the wild cavy in the way he behaves and communicates. The instincts you see in your pet mimic those of guinea pigs in the wild.

Guinea Pig Behavior

To understand guinea pig behavior, you must first realize that guinea pigs are prey animals. In the wild, they live their entire lives constantly on the lookout for larger animals that want to eat them. Each individual guinea pig's ability to be alert, wary and quick is what keeps him alive.

Wild cavies have a number of behaviors that help them avoid predators. In fact, every behavior that guinea pigs possess is designed to help them survive in the wild.

The adage "safety in numbers" applies to the wild cavy, who lives in social groups known as herds. Life in a group provides the guinea pig with security on a couple of levels. First, the more guinea pigs there are, the safer it is for each individual animal. For every guinea pig who lives in the colony, there is another set of eyes scouring the landscape, looking out for enemies. When one guinea pig spies a predator, he signals the others that danger is near.

The burrows of the guinea pig provide another form of protection against predators. Since herds construct a network of different burrows, there are rarely a shortage of holes to dive into when an enemy approaches.

In addition to their instinct of self-protection, guinea pigs also have a set of behaviors that allow them to live peacefully within their community groups. These rules also contribute to the survival of the species, since the stronger, dominant animals are most likely to outlive the lesser members of the herd and go on to reproduce.

Guinea pigs group together for protection and comfort.

Like many other animals that live in groups with members of their own species, guinea pigs follow a complex hierarchy. Each guinea pig herd contains a dominant male and a dominant female, with various other forms of dominance and appeasement in the group.

Communicating with Your Guinea Pig

Your pet guinea pig has not changed much since his species was domesticated thousands of years ago. The

*These plastic
tubes are attrac-
tive to guinea
pigs because they
simulate the
earthen burrows
of the animal's
natural home.*

same instincts present in his ancestors live on in his genes. In order to communicate with your guinea pig and develop a good relationship, you need to understand how these instincts translate into the domestic environment you have created for your pet.

Always remember that guinea pigs are prey animals and are easily frightened. When you sense that your guinea pig is afraid, speak to him in a soft voice and move slowly around it. This will help your guinea pig distinguish you from an attacking predator, who would move quickly and aggressively.

Your guinea pig may appear to be afraid of something or someone that you consider harmless. Try to put yourself in your guinea pig's position. Since he does not have the powers of reason that humans do, he is not able to understand why he shouldn't be afraid of something that we know is innocuous.

Know, too, that your guinea pig's ears are very sensitive because they were designed to be able to detect the sounds of approaching predators. This also makes them sensitive to noises in the human environment. Booming sounds like music, a television or even shouting can drive a guinea pig to distraction. For this reason, noise should be kept to a minimum. The kindest thing a guinea pig owner can do is to create a quiet, soothing atmosphere for his or her pet.

Guinea pigs in the wild create a regular feeding schedule for themselves and stick to it. Given this, the most natural time for your guinea pig to eat is in the morning and evening. Try to provide your pet with breakfast and dinner at the same times every day.

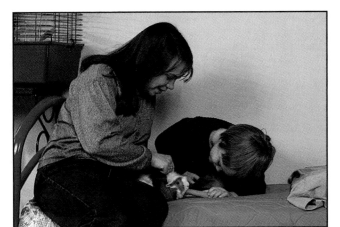

When playing with your guinea pig, avoid making loud noises and sudden movements that will scare your pet.

Keep in mind, also, that young guinea pigs differ from older guinea pigs in their behavior and attitudes. Guinea pigs less than four months old have not reached maturity. This means that they will often behave rambunctiously, much like a puppy or kitten. In the wild, these tendencies would help them learn to cope with life, teaching them to become active in the ways of a guinea pig herd.

Young guinea pigs tend to be particularly active when it comes to chewing and urinating in inappropriate places. Neutering or spaying can help, as can a lot of tolerance and understanding on your part. Patience is key to helping a guinea pig get through this "teenage" period. A more mature and less troublesome adult will undoubtedly emerge.

BODY LANGUAGE

As you spend time with your guinea pig, you will begin to notice that your pet has certain mannerisms and vocalizations that may seem odd. Because guinea pigs communicate with body language and sounds, most of the behaviors you are witnessing are messages about how your guinea pig feels about you and his environment.

Playing Dead   Wild cavies lie motionless on their backs to fool predators into thinking they are dead. They are "playing dead." If your guinea pig becomes extremely frightened when approached by strangers or other pets, you may see him roll over on his back and lie there without moving. This posture is a move designed to squelch the predator's instinct to attack. If your guinea pig assumes this position, reassure him that everything is okay and take him out of the situation that is scaring him.

Guinea pigs may be rambunctious during their younger years. Patience and understanding on your part is the best solution.

Stretching   A stretched-out posture is a relaxed one. Your guinea pig will lengthen his body across the floor and rest quietly. It will be obvious that he is comfortable and at ease.

Stiffened Legs   A guinea pig who is prepared to exert his dominance will rise up with his legs stiffened. This stance usually wards off any advances by other guinea pigs, but if the intruder doesn't back off, a fight may ensue.

Nose Touching   Guinea pigs greet one another by touching noses. This is a friendly gesture, usually reserved for familiar acquaintances.

Jumping   The term "jumping for joy" could have been coined by a guinea pig owner, since this is a typical expression of happiness in guinea pigs. Young guinea pigs are known especially for something called "popcorning," where they leap straight into the air.

Guinea pigs may greet each other by touching noses.

VOCALIZATIONS

Guinea pigs are vocal creatures, and they like to communicate by sound. The average guinea pig makes a wide array of noises, each meant to communicate something to his herdmates—and to humans.

Squealing The squeal of a guinea pig is unmistakable. Its high-pitched sound pierces the air. In the wild, cavies use squealing as a warning to let their herdmates know that a predator is approaching. It is also a sound for pain and fear, and is often a cry for attention. The squeal is also used to beg for food, but only with humans.

Cooing The sweet sound of a mother guinea pig cooing to her babies is very pleasant. Guinea pigs also use this sound to reassure fellow adults. People who have very special relationships with their guinea pigs are also rewarded with cooing sounds.

Teeth Clacking The sound of chattering teeth means "stay away" in guinea pig language. This is a warning extended to other guinea pigs, nosy pets and certain humans. Ignoring this sound can result in a nasty bite from an aggressive guinea pig.

Gurgling The gurgling sound of a happy guinea pig is another reward for special humans. Gurgling is an expression of contentment and happiness. If your guinea pig gurgles at you, you can bet you are doing something right.

chapter 10

Fun

with Your

Guinea Pig

While many people think that guinea pigs are boring creatures who just sit in a cage all day doing nothing, those who keep guinea pigs as pets know this is far from true.

Guinea pigs have gained an undeserved reputation as uninteresting animals because, until recently, they were primarily kept outdoors where they had little human contact. Today, however, many people keep their guinea pigs inside the house where they can interact with people. Even many outdoor guinea pigs now get to spend some time indoors, roaming through the house and bonding with their humans. Given the guinea pig's newfound opportunity to show us what she's all about, it's not surprising that people are discovering what a unique and fascinating pet she really is.

Out-of-Cage Time

Your guinea pig's most basic needs of shelter, food and water can be met inside her cage, but this is just the bare minimum. Your guinea pig needs exercise, companionship and mental and physical stimulation. In order to be a happy, healthy guinea pig, your pet needs regular out-of-cage time every day. She needs this time to exercise, explore her environment and remain stimulated and curious. In addition, you can't enjoy your guinea pig much when she's in her cage. In order to get to know your guinea pig and allow her to get to know you and her home, she'll need to be out of her cage. You got your guinea pig in the first place so you could enjoy her as a pet, right? However, you just can't turn your guinea pig loose in your home and expect everything to be safe. There are a few things you need to keep in mind.

- If you can't supervise your guinea pig at all times when she's out of her cage, make sure she's in a secure area where other pets can't get to her.

- Make the area in which your guinea pig will be playing "guinea pig-proof."

- Be aware of where your guinea pig is at all times. Watch feet, shutting doors and look out before you put anything on the floor in your guinea pig's space.

- Use the time to get to know your guinea pig better.

Playing

In the wild, guinea pigs are playful creatures who love to engage in games. Like their wild ancestors, pet guinea pigs also like to play. Guinea pigs especially love to play with one another. Solitary play is also a popular pastime of guinea pigs, who will happily amuse themselves with simple toys.

The best way to enjoy a guinea pig at play is to give her a toy or let her run loose with a familiar guinea pig companion and then sit back and watch the festivities. Guinea pigs love to run around, leap on and off cardboard boxes, chase each other through tubes and jump over one another. Young guinea pigs also enjoy "popcorning," jumping straight up in the air. Two guinea pigs will sometimes play tug-of-war.

Once they are secure in their surroundings, guinea pigs are playful, friendly animals.

There are a number of household items that make excellent toys for guinea pigs. Try offering your pet any of the following objects: a paper cup, a toilet paper spool, a small cardboard box, straw baskets or a paper grocery bag. Alternate your guinea pig's toys so she doesn't get bored with them.

Traveling with Your Guinea Pig

If you go on a picnic, can you bring your guinea pig with you? What if you are going to visit a relative a couple of hours away? The answer to these questions can be yes, depending on your guinea pig and how you plan to get there.

BY PLANE

Airplane rides are not recommended for guinea pigs unless absolutely necessary. If you are going on vacation and you need to take a plane, your guinea pig would be better off if you left her at home. The reason for this is that most pets on plane rides have to travel in the plane's cargo hold, where temperatures are not controlled. Pets have been known to die of heatstroke while planes are sitting on runways, waiting to take off.

If you have to fly with your guinea pig, book your flight early so you can reserve a space for your pet in the cabin. You will need to purchase a special carrier approved for use inside the cabin of an airplane. You will be expected to keep your guinea pig under the seat in front of you at all times.

If you decide to travel with your guinea pig, make sure you have all the necessary supplies to make the trip a safe and comfortable one.

BY CAR

Car rides are another matter, however. Guinea pigs can ride comfortably in cars on cool days when the traffic is minimal. (They are sensitive to car exhaust.)

Before you travel out of state with your guinea pig, whether by plane or car, check with the veterinary association of the state you are traveling to. Find out if there are restrictions pertaining to pet rodents.

There are individual guinea pigs who enjoy getting out of the house once and a while, and if you take proper precautions, you should be able to keep your traveling guinea pig healthy.

If you want to find out if your guinea pig is one of these adventurous types who enjoys travel, you'll need to get her used to the idea of riding in the car and being out of her usual surroundings.

Start by leaving her travel carrier in a place where she can have as much access to it as possible. Since guinea pigs feel most secure in small enclosures, you'll find that your pet will actually enjoy spending time in her carrier. Place some hay in it to encourage her to visit the carrier often.

Once your guinea pig seems at ease with the carrier, you can start preparing for outings by taking her for short rides in the car. Make sure that you do not take her out on hot days, since guinea pigs are very prone to heatstroke. Wait until the evening for your rides, if possible. Start out by taking short, 20-minute drives and then gradually lengthen your trips. If your guinea pig is the traveling type, she will eventually get used to the routine and will settle down and relax.

Once your guinea pig feels okay about riding in the car, you can try taking her on a short trip. Watch her carefully to see if she seems frightened or anxious when you arrive at your destination. If she is, you may want to reconsider traveling with her.

Their owners know what unique and charming pets guinea pigs are.

If your guinea pig seems comfortable and is enjoying her adventure, then you may have a real traveler on your hands. She may be the type of guinea pig you can take with you when you go to visit friends or spend a day picnicking in the park.

When you are traveling with your guinea pig by car, be sure to take precautions to protect her from the heat. Cover her carrier with a towel to shield out the sun, and use the air conditioner on warm days. Never leave your guinea pig, or any pet for that matter, in a parked car in the heat of the day, even with the windows rolled down. The temperature inside the car can rise quickly, and can kill your guinea pig in a matter of minutes.

Remember also to bring along some of your guinea pig's necessities. A supply of her regular food is a must, including fresh hay, which should be placed in her carrier for her to munch on. Her water bottle and a jug of the water you usually give her are also necessary. (Providing her with familiar water will ensure that she will drink as much as she needs to.) Try to adhere to your normal schedule of feeding so as not to disrupt your guinea pig's system.

STAYING AT HOME

Since new situations often cause stress and anxiety in guinea pigs, and new environments can mean exposure to disease and parasites, many guinea pig owners opt to leave their pets home when they are traveling. These owners will ask a knowledgeable and responsible friend to take care of the guinea pig, or will hire a professional pet-sitter while they are away.

FAVORITE GUINEA PIG TOYS

Guinea pigs are fun-loving pets who appreciate a variety of playthings. Try offering your guinea pig a toilet paper spool, a small cardboard box or a paper grocery bag.

Commercially made toys can be more expensive but just as fun for your guinea pig. Try some colorful plastic tubing that can be fitted together in different shapes, or a play gym sized just for guinea pigs.

Showing

A number of people who start out as pet owners eventually start showing their guinea pigs. Showing can be a fun activity that the entire family can participate in. People who begin by showing a pet often become heavily involved in guinea pigs and end up acquiring a number of animals.

One of the downsides of showing your pet is the pressure it places on her. Showing is stressful for any animal, and guinea pigs are no exception. There is also a greater chance that your pet will contract a contagious disease from another guinea pig at a show.

4-H

If you and your family want to investigate the world of guinea pig shows, you may first want to look into 4-H, an organization created to help children learn about how to care for and exhibit livestock. The American Rabbit Breeders Association, the official organization for guinea pig showing, also sponsors guinea pig shows around the country, which are attended by guinea pig fanciers who are very serious about showing.

4-H, which is short for Head, Heart, Hands and Health, began in the early part of the twentieth century with a community of farmers who wanted to encourage the development of agrarian skills in children. In 1907, it officially became part of the United States Department of Agriculture (USDA).

Since then, the 4-H youth program has grown to be a large national network of local clubs, featuring projects that range from computers to cattle. Guinea pigs have proven to be a very popular 4-H project over the past several decades. 4-H is an excellent way for young guinea pig owners to learn to show guinea pigs and care for them.

Spend time bonding with your guinea pig. This pet is enjoying a good scratch from her owner.

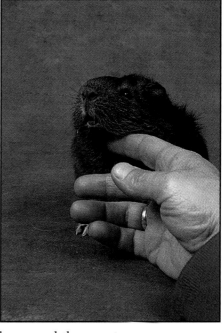

Shows specifically for 4-H guinea pig owners are held around the country. These shows follow the rules and breed standards established by the American Rabbit Breeders Association. 4-H members can also exhibit their guinea pigs at county fairs, since 4-H often has a strong presence at these events.

The mission of 4-H as a whole is to promote farming as a way of life and to help young people develop their potential to learn. There are 4-H clubs around the country, managed by the nation's land-grant universities. General guidelines have been established by the USDA, and individual states follow these rules while

113

establishing their own regulations for clubs in their jurisdictions. The cooperative extension services in each state administers the state's 4-H clubs.

Open to children aged 9–19 (and sometimes younger, depending on the individual club), typical 4-H guinea pig projects feature hands-on learning in a family environment. Children are taught how to feed, care for, handle, groom and show their guinea pigs.

These young ladies have learned good grooming, health and care practices for their pet guinea pigs.

4-H clubs are run by volunteers, usually parents whose children have been involved with the program for some time. Individual 4-H projects, such as guinea pig shows, have leaders as well. These people are usually parents, and tend to be breeders or former breeders who have spent a substantial amount of time showing guinea pigs.

Aside from valuable learning and hands-on experience, members of 4-H guinea pig projects can also earn awards. While actual awards and requirements vary from club to club, typical activities, such as displaying a winning guinea pig-related project in the local 4-H fair or successfully exhibiting a guinea pig at a show, can earn participants medals, ribbons or certificates.

If your child has a guinea pig that is not a purebred, he or she can still show the animal in 4-H under the showmanship class. In showmanship, the exhibitor presents the guinea pig to a judge, demonstrating a knowledge of guinea pig care and anatomy as well as proper handling. Children are graded on their ability to present the animal properly and to understand their pet's overall health. The rules that are followed for showmanship classes are established by the American Rabbit Breeders Association, which also offers these classes.

To obtain information on a local 4-H guinea pig project, contact your county extension office by looking in your telephone directory. For general information about 4-H, contact the National 4-H Council listed in chapter 12.

ARBA

The American Rabbit Breeders Association, or ARBA, which began in the early part of the twentieth century, is the governing body for guinea pig showing and registration in the United States. The ARBA sanctions guinea pig shows around the country. The shows are put on by the American Cavy Breeders Association and its regional guinea pig clubs.

All guinea pigs can be exhibited in the showmanship class.

The ARBA has created a list of rules and regulations for guinea pig shows, and each sanctioned show operates by these rules. Judges who officiate at ARBA shows evaluate the guinea pigs they judge using the breed standards published by the ARBA. Guinea pigs that are exhibited at ARBA shows may be registered with the organization, but this is not mandatory.

Guinea pigs at ARBA shows are judged in classes organized by breed. Within the breed classification, guinea pigs are then divided by age before they are judged. Awards are given to individual class winners, as well as Best of Breed, Best of Opposite Sex (given to the best guinea pig of the opposite sex of the Best of Breed winner), Best of Variety or Group and ultimately, Best in Show. Class winners usually receive a ribbon; Best of Variety or Group, a rosette; Best of Breed, a trophy; and Best in Show, a large trophy. Small cash awards are also given to some of the winners.

When competing in ARBA shows, guinea pigs can also earn "legs" toward their Grand Championship. Three legs qualify a guinea pig as a Grand Champion, which is a distinctive title in the guinea pig world.

REGISTRATION

It is not necessary to register your guinea pig in order to show her. However, many people choose to do so since having a registered guinea pig assures that the animal's pedigree is true and that the guinea pig meets all the requirements of her breed.

In order to register a guinea pig in the purebred classification, the animal needs a three-generation pedigree. The guinea pig must be examined by an official ARBA registrar, who will determine if the guinea pig is eligible for registration. The guinea pig must be six months or older and weigh 32 ounces or more. It must also be free from disqualifications or eliminations as defined by the breed standard.

In order to register a guinea pig, you, as the guinea pig's owner, must be a member of the ARBA. You will also have to pay a fee for registering your animal.

ARBA registrars are present at ARBA-sanctioned shows. To have your guinea pig registered, you must bring the guinea pig and her papers to the show, or make arrangements with a registrar to inspect the guinea pig at the registrar's home. It takes about three weeks to receive your registration papers in the mail once the examination process is complete.

EAR TAGS

If you go to a guinea pig show, you will notice that many guinea pigs have a small metal tag in one ear. You may also see an ARBA registrar putting ear tags on guinea pigs right there at the show.

In order for a guinea pig to be shown at an ARBA show, she must have a metal tag with an identifying number attached to her right ear. When a guinea pig is registered with the ARBA, the registrar places the guinea pig's registration number on a tag, and then attaches the tag to the ear at the time of examination. Many breeders do their own tagging, using a system of letters and numbers that they have created for their record-keeping purposes.

Some people opt not to show their pets since they do not wish to tag their animals. A tag leaves a permanent mark on the guinea pig's ear, and the process causes pain, albeit brief, to the guinea pig.

part four

Beyond the Basics

chapter 11

Recommended Reading

Books

Behrend, Katrin. *Guinea Pigs: A Complete Pet Owner's Manual.* Hauppage, New York: Barron's Educational Series, 1998.

Kelsey-Wood, Dennis. *Guinea Pigs.* Neptune, New Jersey: TFH Publications, 2000.

Lasell, Vicki, and Norita Barrios. *The Complete Book on Taming and Training Your Guinea Pig.* Hermosa Beach, California: Silver Sea Press, 1987.

Richardson, V.C.G. *Diseases of Domestic Guinea Pigs.* Malden, Massachusetts: Blackwell Science, 2000.

Viner, Bradley. *All About Your Guinea Pig.* Hauppage, New York: Barron's Educational Series, 1999.

Magazines

Critters (annual)
Fancy Publications
P.O. Box 6050
Mission Viejo, CA 92690
Publishing office: (949) 855-8822
To subscribe: (800) 361-4132
www.animalnetwork.com

chapter 12

Resources

Clubs

NATIONAL CLUBS

The Guinea Pig Club
P.O. Box 1030
Columbia Station, OH 44028
www.petclubhouse.com/guineapig/
E-mail: snowflake@guineapigclub.com

American Cavy Breeders Association
c/o ACBA
Lenore Gergen, Secretary & Treasurer
16450 Hogan Avenue
Hastings, MN 55033-9576
http://acba.osb-land.com
The ACBA is an organization representing guinea pig breeders in the
United States. Write to the above address for membership information.

REGIONAL CLUBS

Local guinea pig clubs are a great way to meet like-minded cavy enthusiasts. Check with your neighborhood pet store or with a small-animal veterinarian to see if they can recommend a group in your area.

Cavy Capitol of California
116 Madison Avenue
Chula Vista, CA 91910
www.buddies.org

Chesapeake Cavy Club
4112 54th Street
Bladensburg, MD 20710
www.cc-cavyclub.8m.com

Columbine Cavy Club
130 Flower Street
Lakewood, CO 80226
http://lamar.colostate.edu/~kj/

Golden State Cavy Breeders
1360 Sawtooth Drive
Hollister, CA 95023
www.jps.net/bmoon/golden.htm

Hoosier Cavy Fanciers
5123 Kingman Drive
Indianapolis, IN 46226
http://members.tripod.com/~HoosierCavyFanciers/index.html

Houston Area Cavy Club
1302 Dragon Drive
Round Rock, TX 78681
www.thehacc.freservers.com

New York State Cavy Fanciers
301 Beechwood Avenue
Liverpool, NY 13098
www.angelfire.com/ny3nyscf

North Carolina Cavy Breeders Association
4991 Breedlove Road
Glenville, NC 28736
www.getciw.com/nccavy

Oregon Cavy Breeders Society
260 East 31st Avenue
Eugene, OR 97405
www.geocities.com/Heartland/Flats.2618

Utah Cavy Breeders Association
11360 South 1700 East
Sandy, UT 84092-5160
http://members.theglobe.com/cavyclub/ucba

Washington Cavy Fanciers
20217 SE 157th Street
Renton, WA 98059-8212
www.geocities.com/wacafa

Wild Rose Cavy Club
#21 219 90th Avenue, SW
Calgary, Alberta T2J 0A3
Canada
http://wildrosecavyclub.homepage.com

Web Sites

The Internet provides a wealth of information on Guinea Pigs. Visit the Web sites listed below to find out about everything from the general care and nutritional needs of your cavy, to breed specifics and how to show rare Guinea Pigs.

Cavy Care Information Page
www.geocities.com/Heartland/Plains/2517/
This Web site includes extensive information on a variety of topics. Logon to learn which poisonous plants you *must* keep away from your cavy, proper grooming and how to provide them with comfy bedding; and just for fun, visit the Cavy Dictionary to discover some entertaining Guinea Pig terms.

Cavies Galore
www.caviesgalore.com
This adorable Web site offers everything from poetry and songs about Guinea Pigs to online games and chat rooms.

Eva's Cavy Page
www.users.wineasy.se/dan.johansson/eva/mars/
marsvin.htm

Stop by this Web site to view photographs of unusual cavy breeds, find out general care information or to discover the specifics of certain cavy ailments.

Guinea Pig Adoption Network
http://gpan.iol.unh.edu/

This international Web site is dedicated to finding new homes for homeless Guinea Pigs around the world. If you would like to rehome a cavy or have one you need to place, this is the site to visit.

The Guinea Pig Compendium
www.aracnet.com/~seagull/Guineas/

This well-designed Web site is dedicated to promoting the health and longevity of cavies. Stop by to view a detailed care guide, read general articles and search for a veterinarian in your area.

Guinea Pig Rescue Organizations
www.guineapigs.org/html/rescue.html

If you are interested in adopting a rescued cavy, visit this site to view its extensive database. Organizations are listed state by state in the U.S., alongside Canadian and other international contacts.

Oinker Net
www.oinkernet.com/beta.htm

This often-visited site provides slightly time-delayed video footage of cavies in their cages involved in daily behavior. Updated every two minutes, you can even hear piggies talk!

Pig Page 5
www.twics.com/~ward2004/Pigs/pigpage5.htm

This Web page supplies links to a plethora of other Guinea Pig sites. Visit to view photographs and to check out fun features such as "Ask the Cavies," where answers to your questions are provided by three knowledgeable Guinea Pigs.

Video

Pocket Pet Series Videos
S.E.I. Distribution
Pierce-Arrow Productions, Inc.
P.O. Box 6663
Los Ossos, CA 93402
E-mail: info@pocket-pet-series.com
Approximately $19.95